# Managing URBAN SCHOOLS

## Leading from the front

Jim Donnelly

London and Sterling, VA

*To all those who dare to dream*

First published in Great Britain and the United States in 2003 by Kogan Page Limited



120 Pentonville Road
London N1 9JN
UK
www.kogan-page.co.uk

22883 Quicksilver Drive
Sterling VA 20166-2012
USA



ISBN 0 7494 3868 1

---

**British Library Cataloguing-in-Publication Data**

A CIP record for this book is available from the British Library.

---

**Library of Congress Cataloging-in-Publication Data**

Donnelly, Jim.
Managing urban schools : leading from the front / Jim Donnelly.
p. cm.
Includes bibliographical references and index.
ISBN 0-7494-3868-1
1. Urban Schools--Great Britain--Administration. 2. Education, Urban--Social aspects--Great Britain. 3. School management and organization--Great Britain. I. Title.
LC5136.G7 D66 2003
371.2'009173'2--dc21

2002153402

---

Typeset by JS Typesetting Ltd, Wellingborough, Northants
Printed and bound in Great Britain by Clays Ltd, St Ives plc

# CONTENTS

# ACKNOWLEDGEMENTS

I wish to thank Shirley, for her patience and good advice. I would also like to acknowledge the many thousands of pupils and hundreds of teachers who have made being a teacher such a joy and privilege. The inspiration at the start of my teaching career came from the late Vincent McGeown, headteacher of St Augustine's Secondary Modern School in Belfast. The fires he lit then have helped to keep me believing in the importance of education for urban children. The first school in which one teaches is so important for every teacher: I was lucky to start my teaching career in his.

# INTRODUCTION

I have spread my dreams under your feet;
Tread softly because you tread on my dreams.

*He Wishes for the Cloths of Heaven*, W B Yeats

This book is written in the belief that the future of our society depends to a very great extent on how the young people in our urban schools are educated. The vast majority of the adults of the future are currently attending – or, in some cases, not attending – our urban schools. The adults in those schools – especially, but not exclusively, the teachers – can determine to a large extent what our future society will look like. While the influence of the home is probably still the most significant factor for the majority of young people in determining what values the next generation will espouse and practise, in many cases the influence of the school will be greater. This is likely to be the case with the most disadvantaged young people; from society's point of view, these are precisely the young people who are at risk of becoming outsiders in an affluent society. Even where there is strong and positive parental influence, the effects of at least 11 years of compulsory schooling on the minds of young people should not be underestimated.

With the increasing role of urban schools as centres of the community, their influence on parents is also potentially very significant. The days when schools were seen as purveyors of knowledge alone have surely gone. They can be at the heart of developing and modifying the values of the community; in many cases they already do so. Schools can transform society, first by transforming their own school community and then the wider community. They are likely to do this by starting with the parents of their students and then gradually involving the whole community.

In an age when education for life is seen as increasingly important, schools are the experts. They know how to create dynamic teaching and learning environments. They also know the importance of a system of values, shared by all generations and determining the type of community and society in which we all live. They know from experience that educating the whole child – and doing this within the child's community – is more than merely pouring a certain amount of knowledge into an otherwise empty 'vessel'. The whole person is the concern of every teacher in every school and increasingly society is coming to realize how much it depends on schools for that. It could be argued that the effects on the fabric of our society of the period of selfishness, which was the defining characteristic of British society in the last decades of the 20th century, would have been much worse had it not been for schools trying to maintain a sense of community and, one might venture to add, a sense of decency.

## MANAGING TO COPE

Before the introduction of LMS (Local Management of Schools) at the beginning of the 1990s, headteachers were largely administrators. There was limited scope for determining key matters such as who would teach in the school, how many staff there would be, how the buildings would be maintained, and so on. Exceptional headteachers could find ways of increasing their influence on key decisions, but they operated at the margin of influence. For example, they could allocate capitation money and had certain freedom over the nature of the curriculum. However, if a Music teacher left and the school was already at its staffing limit, then they would probably have to remove Music from the curriculum.

Each school would be given a set number of teachers, down to fractions like 0.5, a certain number of hours of administrative support, technician support time (usually only in secondary schools and only for such areas as Science and Technology) and one or more caretakers. A school hoping to acquire new furniture, have some classrooms repainted, carpets replaced and so on, had to make a series of cases to different LEA officers (unless they could be shown to be dangerous).

Once LMS was introduced, there was far more scope for decision making. The idea of headteachers being seen as 'chief executives' led to much discussion of management and management styles. Concepts were introduced from the business world and senior staff in schools spent much time deciding on the 'perfect' team. Every school suddenly started looking at its own senior staff – soon to become the 'senior management team' – and wondered how it could manage without its correct balance of skills and personal characteristics. This developed in both primary and secondary schools.

However, in many schools the reality of LMS in the early years was that senior staff had to learn to manage to cope with new freedoms at the same time as having to cut spending. There is little doubt that schools in general are better managed since key responsibilities for staffing, budgeting and premises management have been delegated to them, but in the early years it was very difficult for some schools to cope.

Now that most schools are indeed coping well with LMS, it is time to look more seriously at the whole notion of leadership. Leadership goes far beyond the ability to administer and even to manage. Key administrative skills can be taught to virtually anyone, while the strategies of managing change, budgets, staff and so on can also be taught to a large proportion of the population. Leadership is a different matter altogether. A good leader can be taught how to be an effective administrator and a good manager through reading, attending courses and being mentored. However, when it comes to the necessary attributes of a school leader, a different approach is necessary. (Later in the book we will look at how society can create a pool of leadership talent, so that all schools can be properly and effectively led in the future.)

## LEADING FROM THE FRONT

The title of this book is *Managing Urban Schools: Leading from the front*. The thesis of the book is that managing is not enough and that school leaders must raise their heads above the parapet if they are to be fully effective. It is no job for 'shrinking violets' and neither is it a job for those who do not have strong convictions. It will also be argued that leadership needs to exist everywhere in the school, and that it is not something that is vested only in the senior management team. Indeed, it is important that the natural leaders among the pupil body are consciously included in any strategy to increase the impact of leadership in the school.

### Theory and practice

The aim of this book is to provoke thought, but also to provide some advice and guidance to those undertaking senior management posts in schools for the first time. It should also be of value to anyone who aspires to lead a school in the future. Some of the advice is inevitably based on the author's own experience. However, much of it is based on observation of other school leaders over a period of 35 years in the profession. It should also be noted that some of the advice may sound like a counsel of perfection: it should not be assumed that the author is any more able to live up to this than others!

## TURNING THINGS ON THEIR HEAD

There are literally thousands of urban schools. However, within this group there are schools – often defined by the term 'inner city' – that are more challenging than the majority. Their students often come from very difficult backgrounds and often have multiple psychological and emotional problems. If the schools fail to break this cycle of failure and despair, then not only will whole generations of children be denied their right to a decent education, but society will also suffer from having a large disaffected group within its midst. It actually makes economic sense for society to invest money in breaking this cycle.

It is recognized by government that these schools need extra support and many of these schools receive enhanced funding. However, a much more radical solution is needed. At present, the way in which teachers and headteachers are paid encourages those looking for their first headship to apply to inner-city schools. Apart from the fact that there will be less competition for such posts, these schools are often smaller than their more comfortable suburban counterparts. This means that the salary on offer is usually much lower.

Once a headteacher has worked in an inner-city school for, say, four to six years they may consider applying for a better paid post in a school where the pupils do not display the same challenging characteristics as many do in inner-city schools. So the way up is to start in the inner-city school and to move out to the suburbs. Apart from anything else, such a move will lead to a higher pension!

It is surely time to consider turning this on its head. The author would argue that inner-city schools need the best and most experienced headteachers. They also need people who will be prepared to devote at least a decade to the job. The way in which this could be achieved is that salaries and levels of support be made far more attractive to experienced headteachers, so that they will see taking on the headship of an inner-city school to be the peak of their careers, not just the bottom rung of a headship career ladder. Put simply, the most difficult schools need the best headteachers. This is not to say that headteachers currently in these posts are not doing a good job. But it does seem rather perverse that UK Education plc does not seek to make the most challenging and difficult jobs the best paid ones. The argument for headteachers should also be applied to staffing at all levels.

## SUPPORTING INNER-CITY SCHOOLS

There are already welcome signs that government recognizes the importance of providing additional support to schools facing challenging circumstances. It is vital that this continues and expands. The economic and social payoff for society as a whole is that the threat of large numbers of hopeless – and quite possibly lawless – hordes threatening its fabric is much less if all our citizens have a decent education and decent life chances.

However, it is not easy and – in the short term – it is not cheap. (In the long run, it will be a lot cheaper than finding the money needed for higher car and buildings' insurance and for the extra police needed to keep order.) As a country we aspire to having at least 50 per cent of our population undertaking higher education. This is much less than many other countries achieve already. For many of our inner-city children, the idea of further education (from age 16–18) is already an impossible ambition. Like other 16-year-olds, they need the support of their family to 'stay on' at school; unlike many other 16-year-olds, there is no family tradition of success in the educational system.

Part of the answer to this problem is to continue to develop many of the activities of the Excellence in Cities initiative, while always remembering that different schools and different communities will respond in different ways and at a different pace to such initiatives. Part of the solution must also be to encourage the best headteachers – and other key staff – to stay in inner-city schools for more than the usual three to six years. A child belongs to several communities – the (extended) family, the school and the local community, among others. If barriers to academic progress are to be removed, the family and the local community must share the aspirations of the school, so that the child's own aspirations are seeded and then helped to full growth. Many adults in our inner-city communities – and, in some cases, whole communities – have learned not to hope for too much, not to dream too much, in case their hopes and dreams come to nought.

It needs to be reiterated: many adults in our society have had a very poor experience of education and for many communities it is not easy to see how further or higher education will have any long-term benefits. In many cases, families and communities have stopped thinking beyond the immediate present.

If a school is to help make a transformation within a community, then its leadership needs to be there for the long haul. The author would suggest that good leadership can make short-term changes to a school in a period of, say, three to five years. However, to make the long-term improvements to the community takes considerably longer. This means keeping continuity at leadership level in the school for long enough to see a generation of success begin to blossom. The very minimum period for this to begin to happen in a lasting way is at least 10 years, and possibly longer.

If our best headteachers, recruited from a pool of experienced headteachers, are to carry out this job, then they need to be supported by breaks – to recharge their batteries, to reflect on good practice, to share experience with others. The difficulty about this is that good leaders in inner-city schools need to be near to the hearts of their schools fairly consistently. Short-term breaks are fine, but long ones may not be. If their leadership is making a difference, then removing it for any period of time ought, logically, to have a negative impact. Possibly, the type of support provided needs to be more clearly defined. Most headteachers have to carry out activities that are at best tedious and at worst energy-sapping. It should be possible to explore in detail the notion of a headteacher-support person to undertake some of these activities, without any preconceived ideas of what such a person would do.

The difficulty of most solutions to problems is that they are not radical enough. The questions to be asked should be, 'What does a headteacher in an inner-city school do that is absolutely vital to the long-term success of the school? What support needs to be provided to ensure that this is all they actually have to do?' Having asked the questions about headteachers, the same questions need to be asked for all functions within the school.

## WHAT DO HEADTEACHERS NEED TO DO?

This book will examine key aspects of headship in urban schools. What will be said applies as much to the small three-teacher primary school as to the large secondary school. We will look at two specific areas. First of all, we will look at the personal qualities needed to run a successful urban school. Secondly, we will look at key activities and functions that such headteachers need to carry out (although not always directly).

### The urban school headteacher – the person

In the following chapters, we will examine in more detail the personal characteristics needed to move beyond survival to success. The arguments put forward will be based on a belief that certain personal qualities are essential and that schools cannot be successful unless they are present in the headteacher. They are also based on a belief that it is more important in an urban school for the headteacher to be highly visible than in many other schools. Leadership of an urban school implies leadership of the community within which the school resides. Parents and other members of urban communities need to feel that what may be among the largest publicly-funded resources in the community (ie the schools) have something to offer them and not just the pupils who happen to attend them.

It will also be argued that an urban school needs to have a simple, but unequivocal, set of values, which are clearly expressed. All employees of the school, without exception, need to espouse these values and to practise them daily within sight of their colleagues and their pupils.

## The urban school headteacher – putting dreams into practice

The second part of the book will look in detail at how the urban school headteacher can turn vision into reality. This will consider such things as how to create a vision, how to delegate responsibilities, how to market the school (and not just 'sell' it), how ICT can help with management and learning and how the physical environment can contribute very considerably to school improvement. There will also be a final chapter on 'Dealing with the enemy'!

### *Not just urban headteachers*

Many headteachers and aspirant headteachers reading this book may well feel that much of what is said applies to their own situation, even if they do not work in an urban school. If the thesis of this book is accepted, many of them will need to, since the top jobs in the future will be in urban schools! In any case, it is hoped that much of what is said in the book will be useful for all headteachers. After all, it would be wrong if only inner-city schools had headteachers with strong visions, allied to strong leadership and management skills!

# THE ROLE OF GOVERNMENT

Unfortunately, the whole process of state education has become highly politicized. This is one of the reasons why we now have a highly centralized – and very publicly accountable – education system in this country. The curriculum is very prescribed, which is ironic in view of the fact that most other countries are moving in the opposite direction! Accountability is oppressive and very public. We have a system of inspection, through OFSTED, which makes short visits to schools every four to six years and then publishes its findings on the World Wide Web. While anonymity may be possible outside the local community for most teachers, the headteacher's name is published (literally) to the whole of the known universe.

If OFSTED does not get one, then the leagues tables do. It is interesting that governments in recent years appear to feel that schools are like football teams (and league tables suggest that being top is the only place to be) and yet no political party is prepared to stand for the election on the platform of openly relegating schools (and, therefore, their young people, their families and their communities) to the second division! To listen to politicians, one might think that everyone can be top of the premiership and that sprinkling a little fairy dust on teachers will mean that all schools will end up with the same points and goal differences.

The nature of politics – in particular, its emphasis on short-term and easily measured goals – is that the system encourages ministers to come into office, throw in some fireworks and then move on to something else. This leaves schools to put out the resulting conflagrations. What schools – and particularly inner-city schools – need is for politicians of all political persuasions to stop kicking education round like a political football. The National Curriculum certainly does not encourage schools to develop young people into 'macho' bullies. However, the political process sends out different messages. Based on over 30 years in city schools, the author would offer the following one set of opinions, followed by one simple deduction:

- Most teachers want young people to do well.
- Most politicians want young people to do well.
- Most parents want young people to do well.
- Most young people want to do well.

There is probably even a definition of 'to do well' on which most of these people could agree. The simple deduction is that it should be possible for the political parties to agree what everybody wants and then let us all – teachers, parents, young people and politicians – get on with providing it.

## Investment

There is increasingly a recognition that a first class service needs to be properly funded. In the long term it is an investment in the future of the country. It is interesting to note that the UK government spending on social security exceeds the combined spending on both education and health. There is scope over time for some of the money invested in education (and, indeed, in health) to have a payback in lower social security spending. The point about investment is that it defers some immediate gains for a future benefit – rather like schools asking pupils to give up some income now to gain qualifications that will lead to higher salaries in the future.

## EVERY DAY A LITTLE BIT BETTER

Although there are occasions on which sudden and dramatic change is necessary, in most schools the best long-term way of approaching improvement is to follow the principle of 'Every day, a little bit better'. There need to be steps along the way and at least an annual renewal of intent, but the only effective change in schools happens bit by bit.

The 21st century is undoubtedly a time of rapid change but trying to be too hasty has twin dangers. First of all, if a significant number of staff cannot cope, then the change will destroy the school rather than improve it. Secondly, if changes are introduced too quickly and they turn out to be wrong, then the education of many young people will suffer as a result. In education, unlike many other areas of business, the impact of error on young people may not be retrievable.

This is not to say that all change is wrong and should be avoided, or even that all staff must be happy with change for it to take place. We will look later in this book at areas where change is needed and where continuous improvement is required. However, change for change's sake is in no one's interest, least of all the young people for whom schools are supposed to exist! There will, of course, be quick changes – such as in the area of ICT – that will benefit all learners. However, even here there is likely to be a lead-in period before such benefits are fully felt.

1

# GETTING ONE'S HEAD AROUND HEADSHIP

It has already been suggested that training can turn very many people into efficient administrators and, even, into effective managers. However, leadership requires more than training: it requires a set of values and beliefs. More than this, it requires that the leader is self-aware and that these values and beliefs do not conflict with the school's (possibly unwritten and/or implicit) own values and beliefs.

It is interesting to note that it is a requirement of becoming designated a specialist college that the governing body notifies the DfES (Department for Education and Skills) of any change of headteacher. The governing body is also required to ensure that new appointees are fully supportive of the particular specialism for which the school is designated. This supports the view that the leadership of the headteacher – and their understanding of the ethos of the school – is of paramount importance.

## WHAT MATTERS TO ME?

Before one considers applying to become a headteacher of a school, potential applicants should examine what it is that matters to them. There are many ways of going about this, but the following is offered as a starting point. It makes sense to write the answers down and, if necessary, to revise them after a further period of reflection.

Many of the questions are of a very personal nature, but it is argued here that headship requires leaders and that the personal qualities of leaders are very important, particularly in urban schools. Teachers cannot hide their personalities from their students, since being a teacher is not a job for automatons. In this country, at least, one's personality will determine to a large extent how effectively one teaches. What is true for teachers in general is even truer for headteachers. Stamina, resilience and self-belief are all necessary qualities in a headteacher. Self-awareness is also essential.

The following questions are in the first person, to make the experience more real. They are not theoretical: they are the first stages in the process of deciding if headship is for a particular individual. Imagine that you are told that you will become headteacher of your present school on Monday and ask yourself these questions:

- ❑ What would I want to change about the atmosphere or climate of the school? If nothing, how would the emphasis change? Would anyone notice a difference?
- ❑ What really matters to me? What guides most of the decisions I take in my life as a whole? Are these things important to my career in teaching? What do I want to achieve in life?
- ❑ What matters to me outside school? What conflicts could arise between these and headship? How significant are they? How would I manage such conflicts?
- ❑ What would I like to be remembered for in life? Does it matter to me what other people think? If not, why not? If yes, whose views matter to me personally – my family's, the teachers', the students', the parents' or somebody else's?
- ❑ What do I think the purpose of this school is? What do I think it should be?
- ❑ What qualities do I think I possess? Would friends and/or acquaintances confirm this? What qualities would I like to possess? Is this feasible and, if so, what am I doing (or going to do) to acquire them?
- ❑ On what kind of issue would I resign from a headship?
- ❑ If I had to sum up the purpose of a school in three to five key words, what would they be?
- ❑ Can I handle justified criticism? Can I handle unjustified criticism?

Answers should initially be written down without taking too much time for consideration. They are for the use of the writer only and therefore total honesty is essential. Hopefully, the outcome will be personal reflection and a renewed sense of self-purpose. It might be useful to look at the answers again in a week or two, revise and formalize them again, and then keep a written copy of them for future reference. It is a matter of personal taste whether one shares them with others. It is worth bearing in mind the words of John Stuart Mill, who said that 'One person with a belief is a social power equal to ninety-nine who have only interests'.

## WHAT MATTERS TO THE SCHOOL?

If it is important to decide what matters to the individual, it is also important that the individual gauges what it is that matters to a particular school. There are several ways of doing this.

First of all, any documentation sent out by the school should be read carefully. Presentation is not everything but it is important. It is worth bearing in mind, though, that the materials sent may have been produced by the present incumbent or by an LEA officer. After appointment, what matters to a headteacher is what the staff, the parents, the governors and the students want from their school. While presentation may not be vital, what is very important is to examine the content of any materials sent. This is where one will be looking for clues to 'big' issues such as ethos and other (equally big) issues such as 'budget deficit'!

Secondly, there is a lot of information on the Internet about achievements (DfES statistics – www.dfes.gov.uk) and how the school appeared to the most recent set of inspectors who paid a visit (via the OFSTED Web site – www.ofsted.gov.uk). Details of examination results and information about the local area in which the school is situated are both freely available on the Internet.

Thirdly, there is anecdotal evidence. However, this should be taken with a pinch of salt. Only if several people, preferably including teachers, parents and students, confirm the same views should they be taken as truly accurate. It takes a school a long time to lose a poor reputation and, on the other hand, some schools with a supposedly good reputation may have lost their capacity for self-improvement some time ago. You need to know what the school is like now and especially what values drive the governors, parents and students.

Fourthly, look for potential. If one wants a reasonably settled school, then one should not take on a school that has recently been the subject of a poor inspection report. However, if one wants a challenge, it is necessary to know not just what the school is like at present, but, more importantly, where a new headteacher could lead it. Will there be support available – moral, professional and financial? Can you relate to the people you meet who are connected with the school? Do people genuinely want improvement and, if so, do they believe that it is possible? Does the Local Education Authority (where applicable) believe that the school has a future?

## THE REWARDS OF THE JOB

The greatest challenges in life bring the greatest rewards. This applies to all headships, but particularly those of urban schools. If one really wants to make a difference to the lives of young people – and, going beyond that, to the community in which they live – there are few greater opportunities available to do precisely that.

Of course, it will not be easy. Sometimes it will be very difficult. However, it is 'do-able' and for those who stick at it there will be the reward of knowing that somebody's life has improved as a result of one's efforts. If one thinks for a moment of one's own school days, the teachers who stand out in the memory are those who blighted one's life or who improved it. The rest are usually forgotten. It is a sobering thought, but still true nonetheless.

It is easy to overestimate the influence of individual teachers, including headteachers, but there is no doubt that it is easier to make a difference to people in a challenging urban school than in a comfortable, well-established one. It is a tremendous position of privilege to be the headteacher of an urban school, in spite of what society may think. The point has already been made that urban headship should be seen as the pinnacle of a career and not as a brief step along a long path of career development.

## ROLES AND RESPONSIBILITIES OF THE HEAD

Every school is different and every headteacher has their own personality. Therefore, the answer to the question, 'What roles and responsibilities should heads take?' will vary from school to school. However, there are certain things that the heads of urban schools need to consider carefully.

First of all, it is likely that parents will expect the headteacher of an urban school to be highly visible. Many of them attended urban schools themselves and some of them had their lives changed as a result of a headteacher's drive and enthusiasm. Many, unfortunately, had a totally different experience. Successful schools are built on teamwork at all levels within the organization, but the headteacher still needs to have a 'presence'. In many urban schools the headteacher will earn considerably more than most of the parents. This will colour the community's view of the headteacher. They will have high expectations of someone who earns so much money. (In more economically favoured areas, of course, the headteacher may not earn as much as many parents, which creates a different situation.)

Secondly, the promotion of the school is important. Local communities will value the presence of the headteacher of the local school, whether it is a small primary or large secondary school, on various local committees. If the school is taking its community ambitions seriously, then it is important that the headteacher or a highly regarded deputy headteacher contributes to this kind of activity.

Thirdly, the heads of all schools have a major responsibility in respect of ethos and vision. (More will be said about this in Chapter 3.)

Fourthly, urban heads need to get a good team around them, analyse its strengths and then delegate effectively. This team may already be in existence, in which case the challenge will be to use its strengths – often long service to the school and deep knowledge of students and their parents – to the benefit of the school.

Fifthly, an effective but flexible management structure needs to be created. How this is done will depend on the particular strengths of those involved. A ready-made solution, carefully prepared before taking up headship, may not be the correct approach. It is only by working with senior colleagues that one will get to know their strengths and their potential. Just because someone has never had responsibility for a particular aspect of school life does not mean that they are incapable of taking it on, with suitable training if needed.

## STYLES OF LEADERSHIP

The good news for aspirant headteachers is that research would appear to suggest that there is no one style of leadership that is essential to successful headship. However, two recent pieces of research do put forward some characteristics that are common to headteachers of successful schools.

A study carried out for the Technology Colleges Trust (Rudd *et al*, 2002: 32) suggests that heads of high-performing specialist schools are described by their staff in a number of ways:

- All displayed strong self-belief, particularly with regard to how to improve the school.
- They were both focused and committed.
- More than half were felt to be unconventional.
- All were described as being approachable and many were seen as risk-takers.
- They were good at securing extra funding.

A study carried out by the Hay Group in partnership with Heads, Teachers and Industry (HTI) (Hay, 2002) identified two significant characteristics of 'breakthrough leaders'. Firstly, they had a greater propensity than average to take calculated – but not reckless – risks to achieve what they believed in. Secondly, they showed an almost complete indifference to externally imposed agendas.

The good news from both studies is that leaders who are clear about what they want – rooted, it would appear, in a strong sense of self-belief in their views – can lead their schools to success.

## SUPPORT

Headteachers need support, both within the school and from outside. Many heads have their own personal assistant or secretary. This is not compulsory! Many heads also hand the management of their diary to this person. This is also not compulsory! The great advantage of headship is that one can decide for oneself what kind of administrative, management or personal support is needed and/or wanted.

In many areas, local headteacher groups offer very strong support to each other, although it has to be said that this is not always the case. Recent initiatives such as Excellence in Cities have meant that some of these support groups are very good and very strong. (Excellence in Cities is a government initiative, which provides extra funding for schools in urban areas. Part of the process of allocating money and meeting targets involves headteachers meeting together to work on such things as reducing exclusions, devising shared programmes for gifted and talented children, agreeing on the location of specialist subject colleges and City Learning Centres.) Such initiatives have helped to offset the 'stand-offs' that sometimes resulted from the element of competition that was introduced into schools when league tables and parental choice were introduced.

Heads in some areas can call upon very good support from the local education authority. Again, this will depend on local circumstances. What looks like good support on paper may be different in reality, of course, so it is important to talk to other heads in the area about this. Sometimes the value of such support will depend on the individual advisers or education officers who cover a particular aspect of educational support.

It is also important to have one's own personal sources of support, which will include family and friends. To this can be added colleagues in similar situations, sometimes in a completely different part of the country. The National College for School Leadership (NCSL) organizes online communities, which can often be a good additional source of support. Professional associations, including the Secondary Heads' Association (SHA) (www.sha.org.uk) and the National Association of Headteachers (NAHT) (www.naht.org.uk), provide various forms of support. These include publications, Web sites, access to local support groups, advice from national officials when there are particular difficulties, courses, and so on.

Every headteacher needs at least one – and preferably more than one – experienced headteacher to turn to when the difficult questions arise. This person may be local or may live in a different part of the country altogether. Some LEAs operate mentoring schemes for new headteachers, whereby an experienced headteacher (possibly from a different geographical part of the area) will provide close support for a newly appointed colleague.

## THE SENIOR MANAGEMENT TEAM

The senior management team has become a well-established feature of schools. (This is becoming increasingly known as the leadership team, particularly since this concept has been enshrined in the pay structure. However, we will use the term 'senior management team' throughout the book as it still appears to be the term most commonly used in schools.) Some thought needs to be given to how the short-term senior management team will be composed and what the headteacher would like to achieve in the longer term.

The team in situ when one takes up post is likely to consist of deputy headteachers (usually one or two, but sometimes more) and assistant headteachers (anything from one to as many as seven or eight). This bit is fairly common practice. What will be different from school to school will be who else belongs to the senior management team. In addition to the deputy and assistant heads, it may also include the business manager/bursar, senior teachers and elected representative teacher(s). It is probably best to review management structures as a whole before making any changes to current practice. (However, one should not wait forever, otherwise the opportunity for change will have disappeared!) To some, being a member of the school senior management team may be very important for status and one's own feeling of worth, just as to some it is important not only to be a deputy headteacher, but to be the *senior* deputy headteacher.

Organizational needs should be the guiding factor in setting up a management structure. It is also important to be aware of any potential changes in the near future, possibly due to retirement. It may also be the case that some members of the senior management team would be quite happy to be removed from the regular cycle of meetings.

For a while in the 1980s and 1990s there was a craze for reading the research on what makes a successful team and then trying to appoint staff to give the 'right' balance. In most schools, this would take a generation to achieve! Sensible reflection suggests that what is important is that the key roles within a team (generating ideas, seeing to detail, ensuring that ideas are feasible, and so on) are taken by somebody at a senior level. There is no reason why someone who generates many good ideas cannot also see to detail. What is important is that everyone on the team sees the value of seeing to detail and contributes their bit to ensuring that it is attended to. It is also important that everyone on the team sees that there is a need to consider the unthinkable at times: this includes trying out something again that may have been perceived to have failed in the past!

Flexibility among team members is absolutely vital. New initiatives come along all the time and a successful team will quickly decide who should do what and what level of support will be needed from other members of the team. There is no one way of organizing a senior management team, but it is worth being at least a little cautious before introducing a completely new way of doing this. It is not essential, for example, to have a deputy headteacher in charge of pastoral matters: what is essential is that it is clear who has the authority to deal with, for example, decisions to exclude pupils from school.

The headteacher with brand-new ideas on organizational structures needs to consider whether the driving force is really a real need to change things or the personal need to be recognized as a 'trailblazer'! Some very radical approaches to school organization have left a trail of devastation when the incumbent headteacher moved on and someone else had to make sense of the resulting chaos. Blazing new trails can be important at times, but sometimes a modification of the present road, with perhaps a few new road signs, may be more useful to the school and its students.

Job descriptions should indicate what additional responsibilities are to be undertaken and should be flexible enough to allow for changing circumstances. It is a useful principle when allocating management points to teaching staff to ensure that it is clear that extra responsibility is attached to the new role. If the school wants to use retention points to keep a member of staff, then it needs to do this and make clear that this is what is being done. Otherwise, some staff will perceive that someone is getting extra money for doing nothing and this will mean that many other post holders will consider following their example.

Another point to consider when allocating and delegating responsibilities is how they will be covered if a key member of the team is missing for a short or long period of time. Back-up systems are not incompatible with effective delegation. They just need to be considered carefully. More will be said in a later chapter about creating leadership at all levels in the school.

# MEETINGS

The nature and frequency of meetings needs to be given some thought. As a general rule, meetings should only be held if they are necessary. It is worth thinking of what economists refer to as 'opportunity cost'. This means that the cost of one thing (for example, the senior management team meeting every morning for 30 minutes before school) is measured in terms of what is given up to achieve it (in this case, no senior staff being available for other staff, students or parents at that time). Some schools compromise by having senior management team meetings before school on two mornings per week, combined possibly with a staff briefing on one of the other days.

It is probably true that some meetings are essential to the successful running of a school. However, many of those held in schools at present probably hinder the process of education – for example, by stoking up discord among staff or at least by using up time that could be spent on preparing lesson materials – rather than helping it. The opportunity cost of having, say, 20 teachers meet for one hour is quite high. The meeting, therefore, needs to have some purpose.

## Cycle of meetings

Many large secondary schools manage with a planned cycle (heads of departments, pastoral heads, tutors, parents' evenings and so on) that involves a maximum of one meeting per week. Many primary schools also operate a 'one meeting per week' system, although the purposes may be different. The point to make here is that if some schools can do this, why can't all schools do it? There does not appear to be any research evidence indicating that successful schools hold more meetings than less successful ones. One's hunch is that the corollary may indeed apply!

A weekly briefing for all staff such as that referred to above – including at least some members of the non-teaching staff – can be very useful, if it is kept to time and contributions are short and snappy. Some schools find a second one useful, but it is probably not productive to hold one every day. (The concept of opportunity cost says that those teachers are giving up something useful to be at the meetings.) If not all teachers are at a briefing

– possibly because some are supervising students – it may be worth considering if anybody needs to be there! It is useful to put a note of points raised at morning briefings on the staff noticeboard, with a note of who can give further details if required. This ensures that all staff can be aware of points that have been raised.

## Purpose of meetings

Every meeting should have a clear purpose. Briefings can be useful for communicating information and for 'testing the water'. The headteacher can raise a topic to check whether there is agreement for a proposed course of action (for example, a request by some staff for an extended tutor period to complete reports) or whether it needs further discussion.

In the past there was often a tradition that meetings of teachers were the opportunity to relive the good old days of university undergraduate debates. While this type of thing may be exciting (or even therapeutic!) for some, it is a waste of time for most people. Very often the main purpose of full staff meetings will be to ensure that decisions are communicated clearly and possible areas of difficulty can be identified. The time is, therefore, being used to check that everyone knows what is going on and are generally in agreement with it. In a busy and active school, it is possible for really significant things to be happening, which involve a smallish number of staff, but of which other staff are unaware.

The other purpose of a full staff meeting is to allow views to be expressed on proposed action or on things that need to be done to take the school forward. Those who are responsible for tabling an agenda item should be responsible for managing it. This will often involve passing round a discussion paper beforehand, and, in many cases, discussing proposals outside the full meeting in advance. It is good practice to publish the agenda at least a day before the meeting and, prior to that, invite items for the agenda from all staff.

The other meetings in the cycle, usually involving groups of staff (for example, heads of department, an ICT working group, a subject department, Year 1 and 2 teachers), will serve different – and differing – purposes. Communication will still form an important part of such meetings, but they need to go beyond this. One's observation of this process for more than 30 years suggests that at least some of the time spent on very low-level administration at subject-based meetings – to take an example – could be better spent on discussing teaching and learning, preparing shared materials, and so on. It is absolutely vital that the chair of these meetings ensures that they are productive and that they seek to take things forward – 'Every day, a little bit better' – rather than becoming a forum for the occasional disaffected person (who ought to have given up teaching a long time ago but lacked the courage to do so) to waste everybody's time complaining about things! A strong sense of common purpose can be the outcome of well-run meetings of groups who often have a shared role in the school. Those who want to moan should organize their own meetings in their own time with those who wish to be there!

The best way of setting out one's stall when charged with the responsibility of leading and chairing meetings is to ensure that there is a clear agenda and that the important items appear first. Any meeting report should be produced promptly and should not be a blow-by-blow account of who said what and how often! A meeting report needs to indicate what was discussed, what the decision was and who is responsible for ensuring that any action is carried out. It is also good practice to circulate the report widely: for example, the report of a meeting of teaching staff should be circulated to all staff, so that they are aware of what is going on.

2

# CREATING A VISION

Even if the school already has a clear philosophy and development plan, the appointment of a new headteacher allows the opportunity for everyone to look at this anew and, at the very least, to go forward with a renewed clarity of purpose and sense of destiny. Such opportunities ought never to be wasted, as they may not occur very often in the history of a school. If the school is not very successful, this process is essential. If it is successful, it is nonetheless important that a line is drawn under its previous achievements and the whole school, with its new leader, sets off towards the future. At the very least, the process of clarifying the vision – and reworking the school development plan – should allow the new leader to inject some energy into the school at an important point in its development.

The results of the exercise can then inform the school's short-, medium- and long-term plans. We will look here at one possible way in which the newly appointed headteacher can go about setting a vision for the school. (This is only one suggestion and it would be surprising if every newly appointed headteacher followed it.)

## WHO SETS THE VISION?

While it is undoubtedly the case that many people need to be involved in the setting of a school vision, it is the author's view that the group to start with is the staff. They are the ones who will deliver the vision.

A second point to make is that the process should not become a long, drawn-out one and that there should be a short period of time between the first meeting with staff and the final document being produced. It is right that parents and governors in particular – and possibly at least some students and members of the wider community – have a say in what is produced. However, trying to please all the people all the time will not work. If a newly appointed headteacher cannot get the process started and completed within the first term of taking up post, then it augurs very poorly for the future.

The vision of the staff, influenced and moderated by the other groups already mentioned, is what will deliver what everyone wants – or not. If it is the former, then most people will be happy most of the time; if it turns out to be the latter, the headteacher will find out soon enough! Sometimes it is a good idea when faced with a problem to let a little time elapse to allow for considered thought. However, in this matter, it is important to remember that students have one chance at education and the appointment of a new headteacher can result in a state of limbo if the new incumbent does not get on with the job. Even the most mature democracies like to have good leaders – schools are no different!

Incidentally, although the process of setting a vision is essential for newly appointed headteachers, it is a useful process for incumbent headteachers to carry out at intervals of, say, between five and seven years. It is perfectly possible for a hitherto effective headteacher to 'go to sleep' after some time in post; the school will suffer as a result.

## STARTING THE PROCESS

If the school has already agreed an INSET date early in the autumn term, then this provides the ideal opportunity to start the process of setting a vision for the future. If there is no date set, then one should be arranged as quickly as possible. Using a date around mid-October gives long enough to make arrangements, and for the new headteacher to make some initial observations of what the school is like in practice.

A good venue is essential, which almost certainly means the best hotel in the area. This achieves two things. First of all, it sends out an important message about how the school values its staff. Secondly, it provides a high-quality environment, in which high-quality aspirations can be set. Very few schools provide the physical environment in which one can aspire to the unbelievable, which is the first step along the way of achieving beyond one's wildest dreams. To look to a new future, it is important to be able to escape for a little while from the reality of the present.

One important decision is whether all staff are to be involved at this stage, or whether one starts the process with the teaching staff only. If it is decided that only teaching staff are involved on this first day, then it is important that there is a session for all non-teaching staff as well. It should ideally be held in the same venue, so that there is no unintended suggestion that some staff are more valuable than others. Each headteacher will have to make their own decision on this, possibly – but not necessarily – guided by existing practice in the school. If the non-teaching staff are involved, then they must feel that they are able to take a full part in the proceedings.

## PLANNING THE DAY

There are different ways in which the day can start. Some headteachers like to show a short video, while others may wish to use a PowerPoint presentation. If it is to be the latter, it should be rich in pictures (or video-clips) of young people who are happy and achieving and should be short on verbiage.

The first exercise should be to carry out a SWOT (Strengths, Weaknesses, Opportunities and Threats) exercise. It should not be assumed that everyone will know what a SWOT exercise is. A simple explanation, followed by a statement of the purpose of the exercise, should be given. The staff should then be put into groups, with a brief to come up with five strengths and five opportunities, and three or four weaknesses and threats. (The rationale for this is that one wants to emphasize that the school already has a lot of strengths and is faced with exciting opportunities. This is likely to be more motivating.)

Experience suggests that some people will have difficulty in distinguishing between strengths and opportunities on the one hand, and weaknesses and threats on the other. The best way of dealing with this is to ensure that group leaders are very clearly briefed in advance. Group leaders should not be members of the senior management team, but rather should be staff who are highly regarded by their colleagues without being cynical. This gives the opportunity for some staff to develop their management skills, given that there are few opportunities in the normal way of things for staff to be involved in doing such activities on a cross-curricular basis. An ideal group size for this kind of exercise is between six and eight members. More than this makes it difficult to ensure that everyone speaks; fewer means that there is less chance of a variety of views being expressed.

Members of the senior management team – and other senior staff – can be used to record the views of staff. It is important for all participants to realize that they should be highly ambitious about the opportunities. This is the time to aspire, to dream, to hope. It is not the time to get bogged down in the detail of how these aspirations will be turned into realities.

Once the groups have had enough time to come up with the necessary points under each heading, then there should be a short plenary session. Before that, the staff who are due to record the findings of groups must ensure that they have completed a short pro-forma that has been devised for the occasion. The emphasis in the short plenary session should be on the short bit! It would seem that, time after time, teachers sit through interminable feedback sessions and yet, faced with the opportunity of doing something more useful, course leaders still repeat the process. What is needed is a flavour of what has been agreed. Maybe each group in turn could be asked for one suggestion under each SWOT heading.

## PRESENTING A SUMMARY OF FINDINGS

It needs to be made clear that all the group summaries will be published to all staff and that a summary of key points (that is, those mentioned by more than one group) will be published as an executive summary. The headteacher is best placed to do this summary. It is a good idea to share it with the senior management team, but there should only be a very short delay between the event and the publication.

A summary should highlight the strengths of the school and the opportunities for improvement. In some cases, there will be some concern about attracting enough students for the school to have a viable future; in others, the concern might be to get a better mix of students than has been the case. The weaknesses should be turned into strengths. If, for example, the school is very good on inclusion but not so focused on achievement, this is the chance to combine them into a forward-looking philosophy. Thus the school will want to meet the needs of all students of all abilities, but will ensure that every one of them will achieve to their own individual potential.

Time should be set aside at a staff meeting to present the findings of the day and to begin to shape the way forward. In some cases, this may involve the school coming up with a short philosophy or 'motto'. This should be between three words and three lines in length! (Any fewer is hard to turn into something meaningful, while anything longer will be forgotten!) If one of the outcomes of the day is that the school does come up with a new three-word philosophy, then it needs to be repeated ad infinitum. It should be said a lot – and if the headteacher feels diffident about doing this, then how will anyone else ever take it on board? And it should feature on school notepaper, internal and external signs, reports of meetings, papers to governors, press releases and so on.

The overall summary should be taken to the governors for approval. It should then be communicated to students and parents at every opportunity. 'Keep it simple and repeat it a lot' should be the guiding philosophy here.

## SCHOOL DEVELOPMENT PLAN (SDP)

In the early days of school development planning, it was not unusual for a deputy headteacher to be given the task of producing the plan. Very often what happened was that everyone was asked to set out what they did and then everything was mixed together to produce something that offended no one and, rather naturally, achieved nothing. It was usually widely circulated and left unread. After a few months, even the deputy headteacher would be hard pushed to remember what was in it. Schools have made progress since then, but it is probably still worth making the point as strongly as possible that a plan that is long is unlikely to be effective. So what does it need to include?

It should start with an overall statement of purpose. The school philosophy should be there, plus a short set of aims. The biggest danger here is to try to include everything in one, overarching statement. This is doomed to failure. The great leaders in history, including leaders of religious movements, have all realized that if something is to guide a person's daily life (in this case, in the school) then it needs to be short and memorable. Something along the lines of 'To provide the best education for every pupil', is a useful starting point. How this will be achieved then needs to follow. Again, this needs to be in the form of short points – for example, through producing well-educated young people, through a curriculum, delivered by staff, using resources. This then allows more specific aims and methods of achieving them to be set out. For example, a definition of what well-educated young people will look like would include the personal qualities, knowledge, skills and qualifications the school would like them to have when they finish their education at the age of 11 or 16, while the curriculum could be broken down into content (including but not limited to the National Curriculum), skills and so on.

This overall template then guides what individual class teachers (of say, Year 3) or subject areas (in, say, Year 8) will do inside and outside the classroom. One advantage of this is that each year when one considers priorities for the following year, it is more likely that 'soft' but vitally important aims (for example, to produce tolerant young people) can be consciously planned for and that they do not get lost in the targets related to SATs and GCSEs.

As part of school development planning, key policies need to be set out. These will serve as a reference source to guide all activities in the school. Again, these need to be short and to the point if they are to have any real impact. There is no need for any policy to be more than one single-sided sheet of A4-sized paper. A statement of principles can be followed by practices, with both sections set out as bullet points. The opportunity cost of producing some school policies is immense and takes away valuable time when staff, both teaching and non-teaching, could be getting on with the real job of educating the adults of the future.

# CREATING THE FUTURE

The future is unlike the past, in that it still awaits creation. Schools can wait for it to happen to them or they can try to mould it, at least in a small fashion, to the way they would like it to be. While the SWOT exercise outline above can be very useful, there are other tools that can also be used. They cannot all be used at once, but certainly they can be fitted into a programme of INSET activities over a period of time. It is a good idea to ensure that at least some INSET activities each year deal with how things could be in the future, rather than always trying to manage the present.

Headteachers always need to be partly rooted in the present and partly looking to the future. Getting the balance right is important but neglecting the future on account of difficulties in the present needs to be avoided. 'Future' thinking should always be done in the best surrounding, preferably with decent food. It is not expensive when one considers the benefits to be gained from activities where all staff become energized and invigorated with the vision of how things might be – or, should one say, *will* be?!

## The school in five years' time

It is very easy to become so concerned with day-to-day detail that one forgets to look to the future. This is where a 'future mapping' exercise can be useful. It can raise one's sights from this year to future years. It can also allow the opportunity to look for external events that may impinge upon the school's future. For example, it is no use planning for growth in pupil numbers, complete with a building programme and a major staff recruitment exercise, if someone already knows that there is a 20 per cent shortfall in pupil numbers in Year 3 of one's main feeder primary schools or there has been a large reduction in births in the area. The former has the potential to affect all the local secondary schools, while the latter may even mean one small primary school having to close.

Another event that all schools may have to start thinking about is what happens when the large numbers of teachers who are now in their 50s reach retirement age. If this happens just as a shortfall in pupil numbers reaches the school, the two events may cancel each other out. On the other hand, the school may be unlucky in that all the teachers about to retire are junior-trained in the primary school or teach one main area of the curriculum in the secondary school.

Of course, any form of prediction of the future is by its nature a guess, but at least the school should be making an *informed* guess. A useful INSET exercise could take the following format. A short presentation is made of what the headteacher knows about present birth trends in the area. If something is also happening on the housing front, this can also be mentioned. It is important, though, not to assume that the construction of new houses automatically means more pupils. If the houses are relatively small, it may be that young couples will move into the area, but move to bigger houses when their children reach the age of seven. This will have implications for both primary and secondary schools.

If other events are known, then they should also be included in the presentation. Following this, groups (using the format suggested already under the vision creation exercise) should look to the future. They should be given a specific date in the future (five years hence will probably be most useful). Questions that will help the thinking and focus the debate include:

- ❑ What do you think the focus on education will be then?
- ❑ What will the school physically look like then?
- ❑ How could teaching and learning have changed by then?
- ❑ What would I like to have happened by then?
- ❑ If I were to create my ideal school for then, what would it look like?
- ❑ What am I looking forward to happening personally by then? (Some sensitivity will be needed here, as some staff may be reluctant to share their personal hopes. However, experience suggests that at least one or two may be happy enough to do so.)

Following this, one could have a short meeting with group leaders and then the headteacher, using a PowerPoint presentation, could present a summary of views. The groups could then be convened for a further (shorter) discussion session, in which the positives are highlighted, using the following questions: 1) What are the opportunities for improvement?; 2) What needs to be done to create the right environment for this to happen?

Following the INSET day, the headteacher and senior management team should take some time to turn the findings into an action plan. Care should be taken to incorporate it into the school development plan at the earliest opportunity. For example, if there is a wish to have an interactive whiteboard in 70 per cent of classrooms in five years' time, then a programme for doing this needs to be planned, including a strategy for obtaining the funding to do so. If staff would all like to have at least one non-teaching support person per class (in a primary school) or one non-teaching support person per department (in a secondary school), again a strategy needs to be devised for getting from the present position (point A) to the desired future position (point B).

This wish list – ambitious but at least largely achievable – should then be shared with staff and governors. It may also be appropriate to share at least parts of it with students, or their representatives: even quite young children are capable of taking many such things on board.

## WHAT IS THE IDEAL SCHOOL?

It is important that not all the attention is given to what the school will look like in five or 10 years' time. After all, the children presently in school are likely to have left long before this idyllic future has arrived. A useful exercise is to work on devising an ideal of what the school should look like now.

The approach here is to work first of all on agreeing what a good school is in general and then work towards ensuring that one's own school meets these standards. Using the group approach on an INSET day, staff should be asked to consider the following questions:

- ❑ What did I like about school when I was a pupil?
- ❑ What do I – or would I – expect from the school for my own children?
- ❑ How could this be summarized into a short set of criteria?
- ❑ What is stopping us from achieving this for the children who attend this school?

Experience suggests that most of the answers will start with such things as the quality of care, the standard of teaching, the enthusiasm of teachers, a range of extra-curricular activities.

A general feedback session will help to get to the key points. Following this, the headteacher and senior management team can devise a short summary of key qualities of a good school. This should be presented to a meeting, or meetings, of staff fairly quickly after the INSET day. The key message to get across is that the staff have produced this ideal for their own children and that they should not aim at anything less for the children who are entrusted to their care. It can be a very powerful way of emphasizing what is really important in a school. It has not been externally imposed and it is very difficult for staff to argue that what is not good enough for their own children is acceptable for somebody else's.

## WHAT MAKES A GOOD TEACHER?

A similar approach can be taken to devising what makes a good teacher. Groups should consider questions along the following lines:

- ❑ Who is the most memorable teacher I ever had?
- ❑ What qualities did they have that made the learning process so good?
- ❑ Who do I respect as a teacher? What makes them so good at teaching? (For this question, it is important to make the point that mention of individual teachers in the present school should be totally anonymous.)
- ❑ What does a good teacher do in the classroom?
- ❑ What does good planning look like?
- ❑ What does good evaluation look like?
- ❑ What is the 'extra mile' to which people often refer?
- ❑ Are good teachers respected? Are they liked? Is there a difference and, if so, does it matter?

The reports back from these group sessions will offer plenty of material for a fairly short statement of what makes a good teacher. This can then be used as a benchmark for all teaching staff. Non-teaching staff may find it of interest also, and they should certainly be involved in the groups that discuss the matter in the first place.

## CUSTOMER CARE

Another useful activity for helping to keep the focus on the pupils is related to 'customer care'. This activity can be divided into two sessions. In the first session, staff should be given the opportunity to consider the whole concept of customer care, in a non-educational environment. Experience suggests that staff very quickly get into what can be a quite heated debate, using the following questions:

- ❑ Think of a time when you bought a good or service with which you were not happy. (Emphasize that this can be anything – for example, the installation of double-glazing, the delivery of a computer – but must not relate to school.) Tell the rest of the group how you felt about this. (Several staff should be given the opportunity to give their examples.)
- ❑ What were the things that annoyed you about what happened?
- ❑ Was the matter resolved and, if so, how? If not, what has happened since?

- ❑ How many people did you tell about it?
- ❑ How many people did you tell about good service? Why not so many? What is the lesson for anyone providing a good or service?
- ❑ If there was a positive outcome, do you feel the same, worse or better about the company concerned? What is the lesson to be learned from this?

Group leaders need to be briefed carefully in advance. They should be told that staff may become quite annoyed as they tell their tales of poor service! They should also be made aware that the general findings about customer care indicate that good service is often not mentioned, while poor service is often repeated to anyone who will listen – and often on more than one occasion. The lesson is that it is much easier to lose a customer from negative publicity than to gain one from good publicity. This may seem unfair, but it is life.

During a coffee break of at least 30 minutes (to allow people to cool down!), the headteacher should meet with the team leaders to agree on the main findings. These should be presented to all staff and, if possible, photocopied for the next session. The next session should address the questions:

- ❑ Who are the school's customers? (Attempts to restrict this to one group should be resisted. The main customers should include the pupils, their parents and the wider community. For many purposes, the main customers will be the parents.)
- ❑ How is the previous discussion relevant to us?
- ❑ Have you had an unpleasant experience with another school? (Experience suggests that there will be plenty of examples!)
- ❑ What annoyed you about how the matter was dealt with?
- ❑ What are the three most important lessons for us to learn about our dealings with parents? (Other groups can be added here.)
- ❑ What kind of customer care charter should we try to produce?
- ❑ Do mistakes always militate against a school? (Group leaders should be made aware of the fact that a temporary lapse in service standards can be the opportunity for the school to actually make a parent even more loyal. It may seem perverse, but it would appear that customers who are disappointed and then mollified often become even more ardent supporters than those who have never had a problem with an organization in the first place!)

Following this INSET activity, the headteacher and senior management team should produce a short but clear summary of what the staff have said they expect a good school to do. The charter should be realistic: for example, a promise to contact a parent on a non-urgent matter within 24 hours is more sensible than claiming that this can always be done by a busy member of staff between two lessons. The charter should then be shared with staff, governors and parents.

The point worth making is that sharing such a charter with parents can help set out clearly what is reasonable and what is not. That means that the school is in charge of the agenda, rather than the 'nuisance parent', who often forgets that a school has to consider the rights of more children than their particular child. The customer is not always right, in spite of what one hears!

## EMBEDDING GOOD IDEAS IN PRACTICE

Within this chapter, several suggestions have been made of ways in which a school can focus on both the present and the future, taking steps forward and improving on the past. It is important that two groups of staff have their attention drawn to the key findings and ambitions, those who are present when the activities are carried out and those who are employed in the future.

One way of doing this is to ensure that the summaries are kept in the annually updated staff handbook. On the first INSET day of the academic year, it is a good idea to issue new handbooks and to go through key points. This reminds present staff and informs new staff of what is important about the school. Thus, attention can be drawn to the qualities of a good school or of good teaching. Staff can be asked to reflect on key points. They should be reminded that these came from the staff of the school and were not externally imposed. It is also worth producing a cover that reinforces key messages: using pictures of happy children working in class from the school itself is always a good idea. This can be done relatively cheaply on an inkjet printer in school.

If there seem to be problems during the year with, for example, service to parents, a short session at a regular staff meeting can use the customer care charter to remind everyone of what the school's aims are in this matter. It is best if this is done in a general way, and individual members of staff should not be called to account in this public way. If only one or two members of staff are causing a problem that is best dealt with by one of the senior management team 'having a quiet word'. An example will make the point. The headteacher may become aware that one or two teachers are causing problems by not completing their registers. This is not the cue for a general moan to all staff, but rather a specific moan to the staff concerned.

## Keeping things fresh

Good schools can lose their way. When this happens, it is often because the person in charge has become complacent, has not noticed things changing, has not constantly tried to look forward. It is vital that headteachers of urban schools in particular do not fall into this trap. The school of which one became headteacher five years ago has changed, partly no doubt on account of one's actions. It is not the same school and it therefore needs a fresh look from time to time. It is useful to sit down every few years and ask oneself the question, 'If I became headteacher of this school tomorrow, what would I try to change?' Then get on with it!

# 3

# CREATING SELF-ESTEEM

It is now fairly well-recognized that young people who have high self-esteem are likely to learn better and be more successful that those who do not value their own abilities or achievements. However, it is not always fully understood that creating self-esteem among young people is only fully successful if the strategy includes – and, indeed, starts with – the adult population of the school community.

One key reason for this is that in this, as with many other school-related ambitions, young people learn from imitating their elders. Some school leaders wonder why young people appear to ignore exhortations, such as 'Be kind to others' or 'We are all equal', despite them being repeated endlessly at school assemblies. Apart from the fact that there is not much evidence that anything said at assembly has the impact on the listeners that the speakers hope, it is important that all those who hope to influence young people are aware that one deed can speak more loudly than a thousand words.

For example, if a headteacher gives a really stirring speech in assembly about acknowledging each other and then is seen to walk past members of staff without showing any sign of acknowledgement to them, impressionable young people will begin to query the value of what has been said a few minutes earlier. This is true of young children, but it is also true of secondary age children as well. Consciously or unconsciously, the listeners will think along the lines: 'The headteacher has a good job and is clearly successful. He ignores "ordinary" teachers. We will do the same.' On the same principle as above – that young people imitate their elders – they will not learn high self-esteem from staff (including teachers) who do not value themselves, or who are not valued by their line managers.

## ONLY THE BEST IS GOOD ENOUGH

If the staff of an urban school show lack of ambition and self-belief, then the process of developing their own sense of self-worth needs to be started with some urgency. In the previous chapter, reference was made to holding important INSET events in the best hotel available. This is a first step to creating the belief that the school will be better tomorrow than it is today. Since every school in the country needs to aim at continuous self-improvement, including those that already believe themselves to be good, so the message here is that it is not only in schools where staff are lacking in self-belief that this work needs to be done.

Of course, school budgets are not limitless, and in many cases they are very restricted indeed. However, if things are to get better, priorities must be set in the budget. The author would suggest that spending on good INSET must have a high priority. If staff are to feel good about themselves – leading the young people in turn to feel good about themselves – then cash must be found to meet these needs.

As the opportunities arise to improve staff facilities – even if this only involves repainting the staff toilets – then they should be taken. Relatively small amounts of money can often yield very positive results. Plumbing in a staffroom water cooler, providing sandwiches and coffee on school-based training days, getting new curtains in the staffroom, are all ways in which the school can indicate that staff are important. A later chapter will deal in more detail with the whole fabric of the building but the point to be made here is that, even within the tightest budget with many conflicting claims, room must always be found for looking after staff during their rest and working time outside the classroom.

There may be difficulties about finding adequate money to do everything one wants, but at least the effort must be made. More importantly, the staff must know that the effort is being made. They then know they are highly valued, even if the school is not always able to provide the level of comfort it would wish to.

## RECOGNITION

One of the most difficult things to do in a busy organization is to ensure that the contribution of everyone is recognized. Many successful leaders manage to find time to write thank-you notes to staff for contributions to the school. In some cases, they argue that this is the most important thing they do. Others do not find it possible to do this on a regular basis. However, all school leaders can do certain key things in this area. If there has been a very successful after-school production involving a lot of staff, a note on the noticeboard congratulating staff is often appreciated.

Comments to individual members of staff are a very effective way of increasing their feeling of being valued, although one must be careful not just to thank those whom one happens to meet on a particular day. Some staff get on with their – very valuable – work on a daily basis without drawing attention to themselves. Opportunities need to be made, say at end-of-term meetings, to thank everyone and to mention specifically that all work is valued, even if the headteacher does not always see it personally. Morning briefings are another useful opportunity to thank staff and to remind them of positive events that have occurred in the school recently. If a complimentary letter is received, or a positive comment is made when the headteacher is talking to a parent or member of the community, this should be conveyed to staff.

One of the difficulties in dealing with the teaching profession is that research indicates that teachers are more sensitive to criticism than some other professions. It is worth working on the principle that all staff working in schools need a lot of encouragement and reinforcement of their value.

Any visit from an LEA officer or adviser is an opportunity for something positive to be passed back to staff. Visitors from other schools, volunteers who help with mentoring or business activities often make complimentary remarks about staff, pupils and the school. Staff do not get bored listening if such compliments are passed on at a briefing or via the staffroom noticeboard.

## PERFORMANCE MANAGEMENT

A good performance management system – which means one that is not linked, either directly or indirectly, to pay – can be a very useful tool in building self-esteem. The problem about this in schools in the past is that the time and other resources were not available to do a decent job on this. When the resources were made available, they were linked very directly to pay. They were also released in an atmosphere that suggested that drastic improvement was needed and that large numbers of teachers needed to be sacked. This is hardly a recipe for improving self-esteem!

If schools are allowed to bring in the best features of performance management, without the aggravation that accompanied its introduction, it may well prove to be one of the most powerful ways of improving the self-esteem of staff and consequently of their pupils

## SUPPORTING STAFF

If all staff are to feel valued, then systems need to be put in place to ensure that they are supported in difficult situations. Sometimes staff who have not been trained as teachers – and sometimes staff who have! – have difficulties with the attitude of one or more pupils. The first way of helping is to provide guidance and training for all staff on the basics of pupil control – Appendix 1 offers an example on advice for all staff on pupil management outside the classroom, for schools to adopt and/or adapt to their own liking.

It is vital that the correct atmosphere is created for staff–pupil interactions. The concept of 'reasonableness' needs to be clear to all staff, so that the school will not find itself in situations where some staff feel they are not being supported in their work. What would a 'reasonable' parent do in a certain situation? What higher standards are expected of school employees, particular teachers, by virtue of their position and their professionalism? These questions are not always easy to answer, but schools that do address them up front find themselves facing fewer staff–pupil problems than those that try to ignore them.

Another way of supporting classroom teachers in particular is to try to ensure that they do not have to cover for absent colleagues. Schools that have achieved this for years have found that not only is morale higher, but staff absence is lower.

### Investors in People

Many schools have found that the Investors in People standards have been a useful tool in leading to improved staff morale. Even if the school decides not to undertake the whole process, it is worth looking at how one would go about achieving the standard and then working towards one's own version of it. It does have the advantage of emphasizing that everyone contributes to the success of an organization and this, in turn, can help make all staff feel valued.

### Opportunities to be together

Many schools find that off-site training opportunities provide a very good way of making staff feel valued, while at the same time helping to promote a feeling of team working. All staff can be invited to, say, a twilight (or overnight residential) session in a good hotel. If they are able to set their own agenda, and if all staff are invited, some very valuable work can be achieved. During such sessions staff will work on a wide range of activities, including preparing additional teaching materials, schemes of work or assessment systems. There is also great demand for opportunities to try out ICT software and to develop general ICT skills.

### All together now

Working at the creation of a climate of success among the staff is only a means to an end, which is the generation of a culture of winning among the pupils. Staff with high self-esteem need to impart this to the young people, so that everyone associated with the school feels proud of this association and looks at ways in which they can all contribute to the success. 'Success breeds success' may sound a little well-worn, but it is true nonetheless. Succeeding together is even better.

## STATISTICS AND OFSTED

Schools nowadays have statistics coming out of their ears! Some of them can be useful, while some of them are contradictory and some are a total waste of time. However, the senior management of the school should use statistics to show improvements where these are happening. Only statistics that are honest (relating school progress to its own situation) should be used. They should also be combined with other indicators, which may in many cases be more important but can often be neglected on account of them being more difficult to produce.

It is nothing short of a national disgrace the way in which examination results, especially in SATs at all key stages, are used by newspapers and some politicians to decry the hard and honest work of thousands of children, teachers and parents. Given that GCSE and A level examinations hardly represent an exact science, despite the fact that they have been built on over a century's experience, it is unbelievable that people can attach such importance to the new and relatively untested SATs.

To say that SATs are relatively worthless is not the same as saying that schools should not improve. Far from it! It does, however, need to be recognized that they are presently doing more harm than good, that they are not really capable of providing any really important information about the education being received by our young people and that they are hampering progress towards the common goals and aspirations of all those who care about future generations.

It is an odd thing that when parents are surveyed about education, they are generally happy with the education their own children are receiving but unhappy with the state of education in general! It would appear that they base their opinions of their own children's education on what they know and see, while they must base their opinion of education in general on what they read and hear.

School leaders should use relevant statistics to encourage staff to ask pertinent questions that will help them improve their practice; and, when the statistics lie, they should not be afraid to say so, loudly, clearly and often. It is much easier to destroy a teacher's or a child's self-confidence and sense of value than to build it up again. Certain elements within society are already doing a bad enough job on the former, without the assistance of the leaders of our schools.

Schools are subject to regular OFSTED inspections. This is not the place to discuss the value for money offered by the present system. At present these inspections are a fact of life and therefore must be viewed as an opportunity for the school. Competent and confident staff will be able to face the rigours of an inspection with more equanimity than those who see something nasty being done to them. It is a chance, particularly for the urban school, to show that one is doing a good job. The vast majority of schools are successful and in every OFSTED report there are opportunities to celebrate success and to draw attention to the good work being done by all the staff of the school.

## SCHOOL ACHIEVEMENT AWARDS

Schools have not asked for the seemingly arbitrary system of 'school achievement awards', whereby schools that are deemed to be successful receive a 'bonus', to be divided among all the staff. Unfortunately, the staff of a school receiving such an award are not allowed to agree to spend it on something for the comfort of all staff, such as new furniture or other facilities for the staffroom. It must be passed to staff in their pay packets.

The school – or, more accurately, the governing body of the school – has to decide how to allocate the award. The money can be divided evenly or on some other basis, such as merit. The wise headteacher advises the governors to choose the former path. If this is done, then it is important that all staff (except, possibly, those with whom competence procedures were being pursued) get a share. If there are, for example, cleaners or catering staff who work solely within the school, even if for an outside contractor, then they should share in the award. The rule of thumb should be, 'Would they have employment rights in the event of a new contractor winning the next contract?' If so, they should count as part of the staff for school achievement award bonuses. There are two main advantages here. The first is that staff who do not earn very much for their usual job can be seen to be important, thus raising their self-esteem. This makes an important point. Secondly, the more the money is handed out to low wage earners, the less the Chancellor gets back in tax!

## AN ACHIEVEMENT SYSTEM FOR PUPILS

Most teachers recognize that encouragement works best and many schools have devised achievement systems to ensure that pupils have something to aim for. In the primary school, with most children being taught by one teacher, this is a fairly straightforward thing to do. If there are two or three year groups, however, an attempt has to be made to ensure that each teacher of, say, Year 5 children is fairly consistent in how they award 'smileys', gold stars, special commendations, and so on.

In the secondary school, it is even more difficult to ensure that the achievement system is consistently and conscientiously applied. If it is not, then the undoubted benefits that can accrue from it will not be seen.

There are several interrelated issues here. When schools introduced such schemes in the past, many staff started with great enthusiasm. They realized that giving out special merits, or whatever, encouraged the children and so they took to it with a real will. However, other staff found it too bothersome, with the result that the pupils quickly realized that it made sense to work harder for some teachers than others.

This led to a second problem. In schools where lots of merits were given, special awards were then given for getting, say, 25 in a term. This was often referred to as a bronze award. This would be followed by a silver award for, say, 50 merits per term and a gold award for 100 merits. Schools soon found that some children could achieve gold awards very quickly, so double golds and platinums were added to the system. Unfortunately, some children were so keen to get these awards that even bronze, gold, silver and platinum divisions were not enough. (A similar thing has happened with credit cards, where a 'gold' card no longer carries the kudos it once did. The author has seen at least one person claim that the card to have is no longer a platinum one, but a black one.)

One other problem arose with these early systems. They became devalued in the eyes of the pupils and, apart from those who will always seek out such awards (and who are probably highly motivated in any case), the enthusiasm for gaining merits lost its attractions. It then ceased to motivate the majority of pupils, which was the object of the exercise in the first place.

A scheme will be outlined here that has worked reasonably well in one secondary school for a decade. It is not perfect and will not suit everybody. However, it gives a starting point for any headteacher who is keen to introduce, or reinvigorate an achievement system in their school. It has been modified over the years and will probably continue to be modified, as circumstances change.

## A cycle of achievement

The system works round four so-called 'Achievement Days' for each academic year. They are always Fridays and happen roughly every seven or eight weeks. The final one of the year is set for about two weeks before the end of the summer term, to allow for the collation of the data. They have also, in recent years, been linked with Attendance Days, with attendance certificates being awarded to those who have achieved at least 95 per cent attendance during the previous cycle. (The end of year attendance date is set for the last day of the summer term, to ensure that attendance certificates are not awarded to pupils who have missed the last two or three weeks of term!)

The principle underlying the Achievement Days is that each pupil can be awarded one merit per subject per cycle. To try to ensure some consistency from teacher to teacher, each subject area is required to set its criteria, which are then conveyed to the pupils. Criteria are set around improvement on one's previous best and most subject areas use criteria such as completion of classwork and homework, and general attitude to work, to allocate merits.

The advantage of one merit per subject per cycle is that staff can manage this, that the merit is worthwhile and that pupils can see the merit has been earned. Subject teachers are encouraged to be positive in awarding merits and the school feels that the system has been an important building block in the creation of an atmosphere where pupils go into classrooms with a belief that they are there to learn. (The first rule of the school is 'You are here to learn'.)

Full-colour A3-sized posters (designed and produced in school, using a basic computer and inkjet printer) are put in every classroom and around the school, reminding pupils of the date of the next Achievement Day, with a motto relating to the importance of working hard to achieve.

## Managing the process

The system needs to be simple for staff to operate. This is achieved by circulating a list of pupils in each of their classes to each teacher. They simply tick against those who are to receive a 'merit'. The opportunity to tick other columns (for example, does not always do homework, shows a poor attitude) and to write comments has been added in recent years. However, for most pupils the teacher merely ticks the merit box or not. The sheets are then handed into the Office for processing.

The merits are put into the form of a spreadsheet, which is then printed off for each tutor to display in their classroom. The pupils can see how they are getting on at a glance.

## Achievement certificates

The next stage in the system is that for every eight merits awarded, an achievement certificate is awarded. Parents are made fully aware of the system and of the dates of Achievement Days. Pupils are encouraged to take the achievement certificates home and many parents have found that they can attach their own 'reward' system to the gaining of these certificates. The school's pupils have become quite good at getting free meals out, cinema tickets, new clothes, and so on, on the strength of the school's achievement system!

The school also awards a notional monetary value to each achievement (and attendance) certificate. The money earned up to the May Achievement Day is given out in June. (The July money is carried forward to the following June.) Although the most that any pupil can earn this way is around £10 per year, the fact that they are highly valued as steps in the learning process, linked to an albeit small monetary reward, has meant that the vast majority of pupils value them. This applies even to Year 10 and 11 pupils. There are occasional prize draws, although the previous system of prize draws, which preceded the monetary reward system, was seen as unfair by many pupils. Some won more than once and some never won at all.

Incidentally, the pastoral staff investigate the cases of those pupils who receive poor comments on the merit sheets or who gain very few merits, contacting parents where necessary. The achievement system therefore in practice gives four additional monitoring points during the year.

## Spreading the word

While consistency of award and its perceived value are key elements in the process, publicity also plays an important part in its success. New posters have to appear regularly in the classrooms, together with motivational slogans, and visitors to the school see one such poster in the entrance hall. The headteacher always makes a point of highlighting the forthcoming Achievement Day at assembly and congratulates pupils after each set of merits has been collected in for processing.

Attention to detail – such as setting and publicizing the days a year in advance, and including them in the pupil school planner – is essential. They carry the same value for pupils as they do for staff. It is sometimes easy to become used to something, and to forget that for every new 11-year-old school entrant, this is the first time they have met the system. It therefore needs to be explained carefully to new pupils in their early days in the school.

It is intended that in future the process will become fully computerized, so that staff only have to tick boxes on a computer screen. It should also shorten the period between the award of the merits and distribution of certificates. At present the data is transferred to a school-devised spreadsheet, which takes a little bit of time to achieve.

Pupils and tutors are also encouraged to report any possible errors and these are then corrected. In a school of, say, 900 pupils with an average of 11 or 12 subjects each, there are potentially in the region of 10,000 merits per cycle, which means that sometimes errors can happen.

Given the desire of parents for regular information about their children's progress, set against the desire of teachers to have some time to teach them, this particular achievement system is a fairly unbureaucratic way of meeting the wishes of both. It is important that an atmosphere is created whereby there is an expectation that teachers will award merits and that pupils will seek to gain them.

There may be some reluctance to attach a monetary value to such awards, in which case vouchers can be awarded instead. However, this particular school found that vouchers, which it used to give, were changed into money by a lot of parents anyway!

It is important that a budget line is created for any achievement system. It can probably be taken from the marketing budget, since hard-working pupils are the most effective way of marketing the school anyway!

# CREATING CONFIDENCE

In addition to a merit or achievement system, there are other ways in which the self-esteem of pupils can be raised. Passing on complimentary remarks through assembly or via personal tutors works as well for pupils as it does for the staff of the school. Many schools use the PSHE (personal, social and health education) programmes of study to do exercises that encourage positive self-image and self-confidence.

The achievements of former pupils afford a further opportunity to spread a 'feel good' factor among the pupils. Pupils should be told regularly that many very successful people have sat on the same seats as them in the same hall. The same goes for all year groups, from chirpy 5-year-olds to possibly less chirpy 16-year olds.

If a local or national celebrity can be encouraged to visit the school, this again can enhance the positive image that it aspires to. Local members of parliament are very often more than happy to come into school: it is worth remembering that Fridays are often the best days for them, on account of parliamentary business.

Some schools arrange to take older pupils offsite, sometimes to a hotel, for activities relating to their future, including their career aspirations. They can be told that successful businesses use the same facilities for their staff, which shows how highly the school values them as pupils.

## School councils and pupil assistants

The formation of school councils affords another opportunity to involve pupils in their school. Age is no barrier to this and, indeed, very many primary schools are at the leading edge of what can be done in this area. It is also possible to involve pupils in real-life work for the school, albeit on a small scale. In one school, a team of 10 pupil assistants supports the teacher-librarian in the resource centre. There is a formal application process, involving responding in writing to an advertised vacancies and being shortlisted for interview. Successful applicants undergo a specific training programme, mentored by an existing assistant. They have regular management meetings, chaired and minuted by the assistants in turn, and they are involved in book-buying trips to wholesalers. This provides the school with a team of very reliable pupils, who have been used on reception at national conferences and who get very favourable reports from their work experience placements.

Once the principle is accepted, then every headteacher will be able to find opportunities to involve pupils more in the running of what is ultimately *their* school.

# 4

# MARKETING THE SCHOOL

Just as no school is perfect, every school has something to celebrate. In some cases, finding cause for celebration may be difficult but if one looks hard enough one will find it. Then it is important to make sure that everyone in the organization knows about it. There is sometimes confusion about the difference between selling and marketing. This chapter will deal with marketing the school, in the sense that there is a product to sell (education), and that the school must ensure that potential buyers (pupils and their parents) are aware of what exactly the school can offer. Selling in this context is part of marketing but is not by any means the only part.

## WHAT DO WE WANT TO MARKET?

One assumes that the school has a clear vision of what it wants to achieve and that most people associated with the school support it. This vision is likely to be set out in a very aspirational way, but with more detail (in the school development plan) of what needs to be done to turn aspirations into reality. Part of doing this is to recognize what the school does well and to ensure that everyone knows about it. This is turn will create the self-confidence to move forward, to improve each day and each year, to get better.

Part of deciding what the school is good at involves deciding what it is not good at. In some cases – perhaps poor achievement in one curriculum area – the school may wish to improve this. But in other cases, the school may have to decide that some of the things it is not good at are not of major concern. It is not easy to be all things to all people and if choice is to mean anything, it means that there may be differences – albeit small ones – between one school and another. One advantage for pupils living in an urban environment is that there may be several schools within travelling distance. A simple matter such as liking a smallish school, rather than a large one, may be a deciding factor when parents and their children are looking for a secondary school. For some parents, it will be important that a primary school has links with its community, which in some cases will mean a faith community. For others, they may want one of their children with particular aptitude in sport to go to a local primary school that has more than one sports specialist on the staff.

Every school has to decide which children it wants to recruit to its school and then make sure that the parents of those children know what they need to know about the school. It may be, for example, that a primary school wants to recruit from its local community and not from further afield. A secondary school may feel the same way. In these cases, this factor will influence their marketing strategy. They will not necessarily want to publicize themselves in national guides to schools. They will certainly have to find ways of getting their message across to the local community or communities in which they are physically situated.

It may be that a secondary school recruits most of the pupils from the local community, but finds that a substantial number go to other schools. It needs to find out why and then decide if it wants to do something about it. If it does wish to attract these pupils, it needs to be clear about the reasons why they go elsewhere and see if they can deal with these reasons. The drift away may be for educational reasons, for social reasons (for example, snobbery), because the parents are unaware of the achievements of the local school, or because another school offers particular strength in some subject area. The reasons for this movement will determine the action the school may wish to take. If parents think there is a problem with teaching, then that needs to be addressed. If it is true, the school must sort it out before they can expect parents to change their decisions; if it is not true, then ways must be found of communicating that message to the prospective parents.

We will look later in this chapter at specific ways in which schools can draw attention to what they do well, but first we need to mention a very important, but often ignored, group of publicists for the school: the pupils.

## WHAT THE PUPILS SAY ABOUT THE SCHOOL

The pupils say more about a school than anyone else – and without necessarily speaking a word! Parents of prospective pupils will look at the children who attend a particular school, whether they are 4-years-old or 14, and form a judgement about the school on this basis.

For older children, particularly by the time they reach secondary school, it is important that they understand two things. The first is that the reputation of the school will affect their lives more than it will affect the lives of the teachers. When they leave and apply for a job, they will have to list the schools they attended. Fairly or not, employers will very often be influenced by the reputation of the school. So the first message they must learn is that it is in their interests that the school keeps, or acquires, a good reputation. The second thing is that how they behave inside and outside school – particularly the latter – will determine to a very large extent what kind of reputation the school will have. Therefore, self-interest alone should mean that the pupils at least want the school to be highly regarded.

Since parents can read about OFSTED reports, examination results, and so on for themselves, the way in which they judge the 'softer' elements of the school will be by observing how pupils behave, towards each other and towards other members of the public. They may decide to sit outside the school for a while before and after school – preferably without drawing attention to themselves – to see how the pupils enter and leave. They will almost certainly make enquiries among any local acquaintances and/or people who live near the school. This presents great opportunities for every pupil in the school to look after their own self-interests! Buses, streets near the school, shopping centres, and so on, are where the school reputation will be won or lost.

## WHAT THE STAFF SAY ABOUT THE SCHOOL

The second group of people who 'sell' the school, wittingly or unwittingly, are the staff. Although the public at large may listen in particular to what teachers say – and how they behave in public (houses!) – all the staff have a part to play. If staff have an issue about the management of the school, or the behaviour of the pupils, it is in the school that they should make their views known, not outside where what is possibly an end-of-day moan can be seen as an indication that the school is on its way downhill.

It is important that any visitors to the school meet staff who are professional-looking (with all the implications this has for teacher dress sense in particular), friendly and purposeful. If someone is waiting in the entrance hall and looks lost, the ethos of the school needs to be such that any passing member of staff will make the simple enquiry, 'Are you being looked after?'

Non-teaching staff play a vital part here as well. Caretakers, for example, will often welcome the chance to wear a proper uniform, provided and paid for by the school. Technicians should also be properly dressed if they are to be taken seriously.

## OPEN EVENINGS AND ORGANIZED VISITS

Many schools operate different systems for encouraging the parents of prospective pupils to see the work of the school. The traditional Open Evening still has its place, particularly at secondary school level, but schools also experiment with open days or weeks. The most effective way of marketing the school to parents who are looking very carefully at where to send their child is to have some form of 'open door' policy. This involves showing them round during a normal working day. Staff need to get used to the idea that parents – and other visitors – are likely to be going round the school any time. Once this idea takes hold, then staff can be relaxed about being seen carrying out their normal work.

On the subject of Open Evenings, it is worth mentioning that parents are far more influenced by the children they meet when they are going round the school than by the headteacher giving the 'speech of all speeches' in the hall. Their reaction to 'the speech' might well be along the lines of, 'They would say that, wouldn't they?' The best advertisement for what the school is about is happy children, who have come back of their own volition in the evening, in order to tell others about how proud they are of their school. (If they are not proud of it, then that needs to be sorted out first!)

Another point to be made about Open Evenings is that many parents are naturally attracted to certain subjects – they may want to see experiments in Science, see a display in PE or hear the band in Music. It is important that all subject teachers understand that they may see fewer parents than others on such an evening, but that each of these parents may be basing their decision about where to send their child on the basis of what they hear in the less 'glamorous' (from the point of view of possible Open Evening activities) subject areas.

It is often very useful for secondary schools to organize pre-visits for children from their local primary schools. These can start as early as Year 5 and are usually intended to give the children a feel for what it is like at secondary school. Sample lessons in Modern Foreign Languages, Science, Technology, Catering and PE are often very popular, since this may be different to what the children know at primary school, probably because of the different resources available. (ICT used to be a big attraction, often because the secondary school was the first place the children could use computers on a regular basis, but many primary schools are now as well equipped in this regard as secondary schools.)

## BIG EVENTS

Musical, artistic and sporting events can have a very high value for a school. First of all, they give the opportunity to showcase talent and to raise self-esteem. Secondly, they can help promote a very positive image of the school.

It is important to consider the logistics of such activities, the purpose of such activities and the likely audience. For example, an after-school talent show will have the purpose of allowing talented children to compete for a prize, but equally importantly to get experience of standing up and performing in front of an audience. In an event like this, the audience will not expect perfection. On the other hand, a large production with invited dignitaries will be expected to be of a high standard.

If the school does decide to mount a large-scale production, it needs to weigh up the costs (including the 'opportunity costs') very carefully. How many staff will be involved? Will they be paid for some or all of rehearsal time? Will staff still be able to carry out their other duties while the show is being prepared? Are costumes needed and, if so, who will make them and how much will they cost (in cash and staff time away from their usual jobs)? What about scenery – who will paint it and when? Who is the audience? Will prospective parents be there? If so, what will they expect to see? If not, is the cost to the school really worth the effort? Is it a good time of the year? Will pupils and staff have time for rehearsals? How much will the event cost on the night (including caretaking and cleaning costs)? Will guests pay or will the tickets be free? Who will organize the numbers expected and who will deal with the sick child (or drunk parent)?

One of the most important questions to be asked is whether the production showcases talent and activities already going on in the school. If it does not, will it create an impression with parents of prospective parents who will be disappointed when their children come to the school? Finally, is it to be a show for the children or is it to be an opportunity for would-be thespians on the staff to show off their talents?

Many primary schools organize whole-school productions towards the end of the autumn term, the preparation for which involves all the pupils and the staff. These can be very successful indeed at raising the self-esteem of the children and allowing parents to become involved in the organization of the event. In secondary schools, it is sometimes more difficult to find a similar opportunity, in view of the many demands of examinations, and so on.

## ADVERTISING

One positive article in the local newspaper is worth dozens of paid advertisements. Schools are often approached by 'good school' guides and the like, trying to sell them advertising space. If the school is trying to attract children from far and wide, they may need to advertise in such tomes. If they are seeking to recruit locally, it is local advertising, press stories in the local newspaper and word of mouth around the community that will largely influence the nature and number of their intake.

A local advertisement about an Open Evening is probably worthwhile, but much more than that is probably a waste of money. Most people assume that advertisements are only telling one side of the story – one does not see advertisements in which schools claim that standards are low or that discipline is poor in their school! This is true in general and very true in the particular case of OFSTED reports.

There is one way in which a school can advertise and gain good publicity at the same time for very little financial outlay, which is to give careful thought to the wording of job advertisements. People may well come across these during the year and a wise school uses the opportunity to put in perhaps a sentence or two, highlighting its strengths. Although the advertisement is aimed primarily at job seekers, those who may be looking for a school for their child in a year or two also read it.

## PRESS PUBLICITY

Apart from some national and regional newspapers that exist purely to alarm and titillate in equal measure, most local newspapers are interested in what is going on in the community. Obviously, crime and bad news will be reported – there are few people who do not read this – but local news editors are usually interested in good news as well. Many of them live in the area and do not have a vested interest in 'rubbishing' it. Nice pictures of children doing productive things help sell newspapers, and not only to their grandparents! The influence of local free newspapers should not be underestimated: they go into every home in their area and most are at least flicked through. A nice picture will often catch the eye of even the most casual reader.

It is worth talking to the local newspaper editor and finding out what kind of stories the newspaper would like to feature. In the event of bad news affecting the school, local newspapers will often present an even-handed picture, provided that both sides talk to them. 'No comment' is not always a good idea.

Information that schools send out in press releases does not always get included in newspapers – after all, it is the editor's newspaper, not the school's. However, that is not a reason to stop sending such news items. Appendix 2 sets out some pointers for preparing press releases, together with an example of a fictitious one.

When articles appear about the school in the local press, they can be photocopied and placed in a few key areas in the school. These can be seen by visitors, but, equally importantly, by staff and pupils. This helps communicate good messages regularly.

Some schools produce their own newspaper or magazine. If the school decides to go down this route, it needs to consider exactly who the newspaper or magazine is aimed at and who is going to exercise quality control over it. It is not very sensible to agree to a pupil newspaper and then suddenly realize that the 'real' press are suddenly interested in the school for the wrong reasons! School newspapers serve different purposes to student 'rag' magazines. Different schools will have different views on what should be in their newspaper, which is fine. What is important, though, is that it knows the intended purpose and is able to defend the finished product.

A good school newspaper can serve two useful functions. Firstly, it can publicize the good work of the school and give all those associated with it a feeling of purpose and enthusiasm. Secondly, it can provide very good training for potential journalists among the pupil population.

## GLOSSY BROCHURES AND ALL THAT

Many schools feel that they must produce a glossy brochure if they are to successfully recruit pupils. This applies to some primary schools as well as many secondary schools. However, some thought needs to be given to spending the marketing budget wisely.

First of all, the marketing budget needs to be agreed. If this does not happen, then the money will be taken from somewhere else and no one will know the real cost of the school's marketing activities. Secondly, the 'customer' needs to be clearly identified. It does appear that many schools forget possibly their most important customers, that is, the parents of their existing pupils. If these parents become involved in marketing the school, this will be far more powerful than any number of glossy brochures.

Some schools have decided to spend money on producing a really nice folder. They then get a print run of 2,000 or more. This reduces the unit cost. Some of these will be needed for the school brochure – produced in house on a decent photocopier – but the others are then used to send information home to parents. (Parents usually appreciate a booklet by the end of September, setting out the outline of courses to be followed, guidance on homework, and so on.) If the folder is laminated, then it can be used in the home, possibly after the original contents have been disposed of! It then becomes an advertisement for the school every time a relative drops in for a coffee or a chat and sees the folder sitting round. It may contain recipes, football pools or whatever, but the outside is doing its job of advertising the school! The folders can also be used when other visitors come to the school and can provide a very effective method of storing documents. They should be used on INSET days – the staff need reminding of the high quality of the school as much as anyone else.

The school folder should say what the school wants to say about itself. It is useful to include pictures of working children, short comments from the OFSTED report, the Web site address, logos, telephone numbers and the school address. It may also include the headteacher's name. After the first few hundred, the rest are relatively cheap to produce. They should be handed round freely. After all, a new one will be produced at the latest every two years, so there is no point in them gathering dust in a cupboard when they could be out there working for the school!

## Headed notepaper

The school should also invest in some good quality headed notepaper. Care needs to be taken over the image to be presented through this medium. Some schools like to cover their notepaper with logos, while others prefer to have one or two selected ones (including the school logo). It is a very good idea to include, among the usual information, the school Web site address.

## Compliment slips

Compliment slips are also a very good way of promoting the school. It is probably best if they are designed to complement the headed notepaper. For both of these, it is worth considering how many colours are to be used. One colour can look well, provided that it is not black, but sometimes schools like to include two or three colours. If a secondary school is a specialist school, it needs to decide if the specialist logo is to be in its intended colour (which may add cost to the process). Thought should be given, especially in smaller schools, to designing their own compliment slips, which can then be printed onto decent paper as needed.

### Business cards

Many schools now use business cards. All staff should be given at least a few of these, since it helps promote the feeling that all are valuable to the school. It is possible to have attractive cards produced, on which individual staff can have their names printed in school. Again, there are software packages available that will allow the school to produce its own business cards. Care needs to be taken to use card of a decent quality, otherwise the school sends out the message that things like that do not matter.

It is essential nowadays for the headteacher to have business cards and a means of storing information from business cards that they will be given at various meetings and during various conferences.

### Franking machines and merchandise

Many schools have franking machines, which offers an opportunity to advertise the school motto every time a letter is sent out. (It is possible to remove these messages if the school does not want a nosy pupil intercepting a letter intended for their parents!) Pens with the school name are surprisingly popular with pupils, who will even sometimes buy them for friends at other schools. Notepads can be sold and/or given out to visitors. These are all part of reinforcing the school's key messages and corporate image. They are far more effective than taking out full-page advertisements in newspapers.

## LETTERS TO PARENTS

Communications with parents – either in the form of a letter or newsletter – present a valuable opportunity to reinforce the values of the school and to involve them in its activities. It is best if they know that they can expect a letter, even if it is on a termly basis, than to be uncertain about when the next one will arrive. It is useful, in the secondary school at least, to send out one letter in the post each year (possibly in August), in which parents can then be told when to receive further communications. Even this is not foolproof, but it is better than pupil post!

It is worth viewing every essential letter to parents – for example, announcing an early finish at the end of term or even closing the school for a day on account of heating problems – as an opportunity to communicate other matters to the parents at the same time. Any extra information included in the letter will not cost any more in terms of photocopying or paper.

## SCHOOL WEB SITE

A good Web site is a very cost-effective way of promoting the school, to prospective pupils and their parents, the community at large, prospective employees and former pupils (from every corner of the globe). Thought needs to be given to deciding:

- What is the 'feel' of the Web site to be like?
- Who is going to be responsible for its 'editorial' control?
- Who and how is it going to be regularly updated?
- Who is going to reply to e-mails?

Schools sometimes get involved in the excitement of producing a Web site, without giving attention to the four points listed. This is a mistake, as what can be a potentially powerful tool for promoting the school then becomes a liability.

It is, of course, possible to have more than one school Web site, serving different purposes for different audiences. An alternative to this is to have one main 'welcome page', which then leads to other areas that may look and feel different to each other: one area might be for prospective parents, another for existing parents, another for former pupils, and so on.

### The 'feel' of the Web site

Some schools present a Web site that looks very similar to an online school brochure. It has been professionally produced and is designed to have a 'glossy' feel to it. Important information, such as one finds in a school brochure, is presented. The advantage of the Web site here is that it is possible to present much more information for virtually no extra cost, unlike printed brochures, which are very expensive indeed.

If the school decides to do this, it is important to ensure that the Web site will look well, not only on the latest, highly-specified computer, but also on a computer that is not as good as this. Schools sometimes use a file format that allows readers to print sheets off on their computer at home in a style that looks similar to that intended. Unlike the printed brochure, which looks the same whoever picks it up, the Web site can look different and, in some cases, less 'glossy'. Professional advice should be sought on this matter by the school that decides to go for the 'glossy brochure' approach.

Other schools have decided to go for a 'pupils at work' type of approach. This is particularly the case with primary school Web sites, but there is no reason why secondary schools cannot adopt this approach as well. Sometimes 'soft' marketing can be more effective that 'hard' marketing.

In a 'pupils at work' Web site, there will be news items about school events, very often with pictures. The advice generally given to schools about photos of pupils (and possibly of staff) is that full names should not appear alongside photos. The key point is that a stranger should not be able to find out something about a child just by looking at the school Web site. In the case of children whose identity is not to be released to specific people (for example, an estranged parent who is a danger to the child and/or the parent with whom the child is living), it is important that neither their picture nor their name appears.

## Who should 'edit' the school Web site?

School Web sites are very easy to set up. If a school is finding it difficult, there is likely to be a child who will show how it can be done! (Many school children have their own personal Web sites. Teachers are probably best advised not to go looking for these!)

One downside of this ease of 'publishing' is that spelling mistakes, 'unhelpful' comments, and so on can appear very quickly. Often the first that the headteacher will know about something embarrassing being on the school Web site is when a parent (or, potentially worse, the local press) calls the school with the details.

If the headteacher does not wish to get involved in the editorial side of things, then it must be clear who is going to take responsibility. One major role will be to ensure that any problems that do arise are sorted out promptly. A Web site is active 24/7, to use the jargon. This means that every moment of every day, someone may be reading what that school is saying about itself.

## Updating the school Web site

One major difficulty for everyone with a Web site is keeping it up to date. A decision needs to be taken on how often the Web site will be updated and then how this will be communicated to visitors to the site.

It makes a certain amount of sense for schools to aim at a weekly update. On the welcome page, it therefore needs to say something like: 'Welcome to the Friendly Town High School Web site. We aim to update this site weekly during term time. It was last updated on. . .'. People who wish to visit the site regularly then know what to expect and how often to check for changes. Many schools find that former pupils of the school like to know how it is getting on and sometimes use it as a way of getting in contact with old school friends whom they may not have seen for 40 or 50 years. (Absence does appear to make the heart grow fonder in this area of school life!)

## Replying to e-mails

The school Web site should have an address for any e-mails. This should be a dedicated address, so that it is clear what prompted the e-mails. Something along the lines of 'Website@FriendlyHighSchool.com' serves this purpose. It needs to be made clear on the Web site that instant replies are not necessarily going to follow. A weekly check on this e-mail address should be adequate. (Parents need to know that they should not, therefore, send a message that they cannot attend this evening's parent event!)

There are likely to be several types of message received directly via the Web site e-mail link. The first will be from present and/or former pupils and parents. In most cases, these will be along the lines of, 'Have just come across the school Web site and am very pleased to see how well it looks'. A short reply to this is usually all that is needed.

Another type of message may be asking for information about the school. It may be a good idea to ask for an address, to which a paper copy of the school prospectus can be sent. If the correspondent is not willing to divulge this information, then the correspondence should be terminated at this point.

All those with Web sites and e-mail addresses are considered fair game for what is referred to as 'spam'. This is the equivalent of junk mail and junk faxes. They are very easy and cheap to send out, and are a thorough nuisance to recipients. The following advice is offered. Never open an attachment to an e-mail, unless you know who has sent it. Do not reply to the note, 'If you wish to be removed from this mailing list, please e-mail us'. In many cases, all you do is confirm that the e-mail account is 'active', that is, it is being checked on a regular basis. The easiest thing to do is to delete the message. If it appears again, consider blocking it, using relevant e-mail software. Another type of e-mail may be abusive, either about the school or about somebody who works there. One can either delete it or notify the police in nasty cases.

From the above discussion, it will be fairly apparent that the responsibility for checking these e-mails should not be left to pupils. If the headteacher does not wish to do this, then it is should be delegated to a senior person – possibly a teacher, a system manager or a senior administrative officer – with clear direction on how to deal with them.

# 5

# THE PEOPLE TO DO THE JOB

One of the most important responsibilities of the headteacher of any school, but particularly of an urban school, is to ensure that the right staff are appointed and that they are then trained regularly to do their job effectively. If the right staff are in place and are on top of their jobs, the headteacher can spend more time looking to the future, thus ensuring that present good practice does not become the only show in town.

## CREATING LEADERSHIP AT ALL LEVELS

It is not entirely a coincidence that great playwrights and great musicians appear in clusters. They appear in times and circumstances that are right for all playwrights and all musicians. It can be the same for leadership. Good leadership at a senior level in a school should encourage the growth and development of leadership at all levels. Attention should be paid to creating an environment in which many staff will be moved to do what leaders do, namely try things out, make mistakes, try other things and – more than anything else – keep going. The government is, rather belatedly, finding out that leaders work within an environment in which you do not tell them what to do, but what needs to be done.

All potential leaders in the school need to have four things clear in their minds. First of all, they need to believe that the education of the young is extremely important. Secondly, they need to know – possibly paradoxically, given the message of this book – that schooling is not the most important thing in life. Thirdly, they need to realize that they will not be pilloried for failure, provided that they have tried. It is only by encouraging the risk-takers that poor – or, even, good – will get better. Fourthly, they need to be able to shoulder responsibility and to work with their colleagues on ensuring that challenges are overcome. Members of the senior management team, in particular, need to ensure that they do not try to undermine the efforts of the team.

## Hierarchy

A major obstacle to the exercise of positive leadership at all levels within an organization is the notion of hierarchy. Those who have given long service to a school deserve to have this fact recognized. If they continue to push the boundaries, they also deserve to have this recognized. However, good ideas are not the sole province of senior management within any organization, least of all within as inherently a conservative one such as a school. The challenge for the headteacher is to create a proper sense of respect for each other and an orderly, calm atmosphere. Within this, all ideas should be welcomed, whoever brings them forward.

One vital thing is to ensure that 'half-baked' ideas are allowed to appear. If people feel that they can 'think out loud', then they are more likely to come up with something truly innovative. The right atmosphere allows the germ of ideas to develop. It does not matter who has been involved from the beginning to the end of the process: the end result should be something of which everybody claims a share. The point needs to be made again and again: one cannot force people to innovate, one can only create the breeding ground for innovation.

Differentials in salary scales need not be a barrier to generating multi-level leadership. A key to doing this is to ensure that everyone within the organization knows that extra pay – including for the position of head-teacher – implies that some people have to take on more responsibility than others. It does not imply that the best paid are better than the others.

# THINK TANKS

Some schools find that 'think tanks' produce very worthwhile results. This can be set up by inviting any staff – teaching and non-teaching – to take part in an offsite event, with a particular theme. This might be about where the school hopes to be in five years' time or how something new will be introduced into the curriculum. The specific role of such a group is not to come up with solutions to anything: their role is to come up with ideas. Sometimes the ideas generated at such an activity will bear little – or, even, no! – relation to the intended purpose. This is in the nature of idea generation. Successful variations on the theme can include twilight and/or residential activities. They could also include booking a carriage on a train, especially since train journeys are very often long enough to do a lot of work!

All staff should be encouraged to jot down any ideas or proposals, relating to any aspect of school life, with a view to passing them to a member of the senior management team for consideration. The school needs to be always on the lookout for ideas, even in embryonic form. Anyone may come up with the germ of an idea that leads to the school improving.

Once this kind of atmosphere has been created, the headteacher will be surprised at how often someone will come up with a totally new 'take' on something. It is particularly noticeable that some of these ideas are not directly linked to the idea-generator's role in the school. It is important that all staff understand that the fact that an idea is generated elsewhere does not imply criticism of the person whose normal job it is to manage that aspect of the school's activities.

## Not only paid staff

Good ideas need not come only from paid staff – or from adults. In many cases some very useful suggestions come from pupils, some of whom are very young indeed. It is an observable phenomenon that some children show 'natural' leadership qualities even before they start school. Encouraging leadership should extend to all, thus maximizing the chances of finding really good ideas.

It is important that anyone generating an idea understands that not every idea, even a very good one, is acted upon. This is in the nature of life. However, some ideas will be put into practice, particularly those where everyone says, 'Why didn't we think of this before?' Here are a few examples:

- A school decided to introduce extra literacy lessons for Year 7 and 8 pupils. So as not to disrupt lessons, it was agreed that they should be held before school, during lunchtimes and after school. Would the children turn up? A letter was drafted, asking for parental permission. However, it was decided to approach it differently. The letter to parents was rewritten, suggesting that this was free extra tuition and setting out when their children would be involved. They were asked to sign up to this and everyone did so. A simple device of wording a letter in a certain way gained extra teaching time.
- The recruitment of midday supervisors can be difficult. One school helped solve the problem when it next had a vacancy for a caretaker by including midday supervision in the duties and by recruiting someone who had the skills and personality to do this.

- The Art department needed some technician support but there was not enough budget for more than about 12 hours per week. Instead of trying to find an individual who would do this, it was decided to do a job analysis first. It was realized at this point that such a person would not necessarily be needed during normal school hours. Two ex-pupils – who were taking advanced courses in Art in a further education college – were recruited to work six hours each. Not only did the work get done, but also the new recruits set a role model for other pupils in the school.

## WHAT STAFF DOES A SCHOOL NEED?

It is fairly obvious that a school will employ teachers. In fact, when the author first started teaching, the school had about 40 teachers, one caretaker, one secretary and (presumably) a couple of cleaners! Nowadays, the situation is much different. A trend towards the employment of extra teaching assistants and administrative staff appeared to accelerate with the introduction of LMS (Local Management of Schools). Recent moves have raised the whole notion of what a teacher should do and what should be passed onto others to do.

The notion is now very much that the teacher manages learning: identifying the learning needs of pupils, preparing learning materials, ensuring that they are delivered and then managing the assessment of progress. Some suggestions are more than a bit unrealistic but in general it appears that the idea of the teacher as a professional, supported by other experts, will be the principle paradigm for the immediate and medium-term future. This should enhance the standing of teachers, but it should enhance the role of various non-teaching staff in schools at the same time.

A few things are worth saying about the various staff who are now under the management of the headteacher of any size of school.

### Administrative support

In many small schools, there is one 'secretary', who acts as bursar, personal assistant to the headteacher, receptionist, telephonist, typist, photocopying expert and friend to everyone (including sick children). In larger schools, some of these roles are filled by different people, thus allowing for the development of specialist roles and, in some cases, the creation of a career structure for school administrative staff. In larger schools, it is often a requirement of auditors that some financial responsibilities – for example, placing orders and paying invoices – are done by different people. (Sometimes this can be taken to ridiculous extremes. It is an interesting question – if one person can do both in a small school, because they only have one person, why is it such problem in a larger school?)

The headteacher in a larger school has to decide whether to have a business manager, a bursar, a personal assistant, an office manager, a reprographics' specialist, and so on, or just some of these. There is no right answer to this, of course, but the following points are worthy of consideration.

The first thing is that any job description needs to be flexible for changing circumstances. Hardly anyone used a computer in school offices a decade ago, and now everyone does. Job descriptions had to change to allow this to happen. Although this was a drastic change, there are many changes that occur on an incremental basis in any school. This means that staff need to be willing to change what they are doing, with additional training if necessary.

Secondly, the appointment of a new headteacher is often seen as an opportunity to make a bid for a central role in the operation of what is still often referred to as the 'school office'. The sensible newcomer will 'play a dead bat' to all of this and wait until there has been the opportunity to evaluate the needs of the school and the strengths of the staff before making any major decisions. It is good to let staff know that this process is being undertaken. It is also a good idea to put a timescale in place, by which time staff will be informed about any changes to the structure and will be invited to discuss any concerns (or, indeed, hopes) that they have.

Line management responsibilities become quite important as the number of administrative support employees grows. It may be appropriate in some cases for joint line management to be shared between an office or business manager for general work, but with responsibility for, say, all pastoral letters, reporting to a deputy headteacher. Staff who sometimes have conflicting claims being made on them need someone who can make decisions about which things are to be main priorities.

## Technician support

All schools need some kind of ICT (Information and Communication Technology) technician support. The exact nature of such support will vary, particularly with the size of the school and the proportion of the school budget that is spent on ICT. A large secondary school may have one or more full-time ICT technicians, with the possibility of one of them being designated as network manager and the other looking after non-networked computers.

For smaller schools, a favoured solution is a shared technician. If five schools share one technician, then they can have one day a week (or its equivalent) of support. Unless the network becomes non-operational, many of the jobs that have to be done are not too urgent. A good money- (and aggravation-) saving tip is to try to increase the amount of work stored on the network (including pupil work) and to minimize the amount of printing that is done. This can minimize the printer problems that seem to arise more frequently than any others in the ICT area.

Secondary schools also traditionally have one or more technicians to support the teaching of Science and of Technology. Many schools are now moving towards an enhanced role, which includes supporting pupils or teachers in laboratories and workshops. It is also the case that many schools are realizing that there is little financial gain in employing technicians on a term-time only basis, when the allowance for holiday pay is taken into consideration. Provided that teachers are properly organized, there is much useful work that can be done by technicians during the holiday periods.

## Classroom assistants

There are two main types of classroom assistant in schools. The first ones concentrate mainly on supporting children, often on a one-to-one basis. The others concentrate on supporting teachers.

Traditionally, primary schools have been more likely to have classroom assistants in any great numbers, but it is becoming more common for secondary schools to have them as well. Some quite imaginative ways are being found of supporting the teaching function. There is a move towards one support assistant per class in primary schools, with one per subject department in secondary schools. Such staff can provide extra support for pupils and another pair of hands (and eyes!) for teachers. They can also undertake some of the administrative duties, even to the point of making brief records of lessons taught, stock control, issuing books, and so on. A former pupil studying A level may be able to help with a Key Stage 3 or 4 class on days when they are not at college, including preparing additional support materials for the teacher. Many secondary school pupils spend perhaps half a day per week on attachment to local primary and special schools.

The introduction of learning mentors into schools has been one of the greatest and most effective innovations of recent years. When recruiting them, it is important to ensure that they add to existing provision. Their role needs to be clearly defined. In particular, they are not classroom assistants. Properly handled, the presence of learning mentors in schools is already transforming the life chances of large numbers of city children.

## Staff working for contractors

Schools should not forget the staff who, while being under contract to an outside firm (for example, as part of a catering or cleaning contract), are likely to have employment rights in the school in the event of the firm losing a contract. They are different to people who work for one of the school's contractors (grounds maintenance might be a good example), but who work in different places. Given that the first group of staff do have employment rights with the school and that for many of them it is their only job, it makes sense to consider them as part of the school staff for as many purposes as possible.

Although some of the staff concerned may only work at the school for a short period of time, it is interesting to see how many have been in the school for a considerable period of time. They are often unnoticed, particularly if they only work in the school before and after normal working hours.

## Site managers

More will be said about caretaking and premises management in a later chapter, but here it is worth noting that old-fashioned caretaking is being replaced by one or more staff who can carry out caretaking, painting, plumbing, pupil supervision, security, and so on. This can sometimes mean that the school can afford to employ an extra caretaker (using money saved on routine repairs, midday supervision and/or lettings). This in turn may mean that the school can stay open later, reducing the cost of putting on, say, parent-toddler classes or study support for older pupils.

It is important that line management issues are dealt with clearly. In some schools the business manager carries out this function, while other schools have a site manager. Sometimes the latter is the former caretaker with added responsibilities, allied with a higher salary and appropriate training. If the decision to move along this route is made, care needs to be taken to ensure that the school gets a clear return on redesignation and salary upgrading. It is no use if the same person with a different title does not commit fully to the school vision and does not take responsibilities seriously.

# THE MANAGEMENT BURDEN

It is important for headteachers to realize that employing extra staff, whether teaching or non-teaching, carries with it an additional management burden. While a headteacher with up to 40 staff may be able to meet them all to discuss their professional development on an annual basis, it may be unrealistic for a headteacher with around 200 staff to do so. If one only counts the number of teachers in the school, there is the danger of forgetting that there may be nearly as many employees again under the direct or indirect supervision of the school.

Members of the senior management team can be used to carry out some of these vital staff support roles. However, they need to be carefully selected, if they are to provide not only a friendly ear but also a positive role model. One has to be careful not to put the cynic in charge of the enthusiastic young staff that every school needs. That is akin to putting an arsonist in charge of the local fire station.

## STAFF RECRUITMENT

Successful businesses take the view that well-trained staff are a benefit to their organizations. This is true even when they sometimes then leave to go for promotion elsewhere. The strength of this argument is that an organization will attract better staff if it has a good reputation for staff training. This argument applies equally in schools.

The best form of recruitment is by word of mouth. If a school gets a good reputation, then it will find it easier to recruit staff. There are a number of other points worth making.

When sending out materials to candidates, it makes an important point if a general information leaflet is sent out to all potential employees. It needs to be made clear that this is the case, as it makes an important point about how all staff are valued. It should not be automatically assumed that a potential caretaker will not be interested in the overall school vision, the number of pupils on roll, and even the nature of the curriculum.

Advertising for teachers is usually done on a national basis, using the *Times Educational Supplement* (*TES*) and/or some national dailies that carry educational recruitment sections. Online advertising is now possible also, in which case the school needs to be prepared to receive applications from around the world. A decision has to be taken on how to deal with e-mail enquiries. Some schools e-mail the normal details as an attachment, inviting applicants to submit a curriculum vitae and a letter of application. (If this is done it is important to set out some questions to be addressed in the application letter.) Online recruiting is in its infancy, but is set to grow in importance. Schools need to prepare themselves for this way of recruiting. It is interesting to note that every vacancy advertised in the *TES* each week also appears on its Web site.

It is worth considering having student teachers, in manageable numbers, on BEd and PGCE courses. This can help urban schools recruit teachers who might otherwise believe all they hear about 'blackboard jungles'. Student teachers get a chance to look at the school and the school gets a chance to look at them. Many urban schools are fully staffed only because of this kind of link.

Advertising for staff other than teachers is usually done on a local basis. In this case, schools should expect to receive enquiries through local job centres and recruitment services, possibly before the job advertisement appears in the press.

One final point worth making is that if someone takes the time to apply for a post in a school, it should be automatic policy to let them know if they have got the job or not. If the cost of doing so is counted as marketing, then it will seem a lot cheaper than if it merely counts as postage costs!

# 6

# PROMOTING LEARNING

The best teams are all clear about the nature of the game. They know the difference between football and cricket. They know what they need to do to win and then they set about doing precisely that. Schools need to be every bit as clear about the nature of their game, which is learning. At different points in the history of schooling, some schools have become distracted from their core purpose and have become involved in areas that are more appropriately the province of social services, government, and so on.

Schools do become involved with trying to remove barriers to learning, but it is important that boundaries of responsibility and activity are defined. There are occasions when young people are so distressed that learning is impossible. On these occasions, it is clearly important that these barriers are removed and the school can help to do this. The provision of learning mentors in many urban secondary schools and, hopefully, the extension of this to primary schools can help considerably with creating the right conditions for children to learn.

However, there comes a point at which the school has got to say that it is someone else's responsibility: if there is a serious problem in the child's home, then it is not ultimately the school that needs to sort it out. Schools can – and, indeed, should – alert the appropriate agencies when they come across situations that need external intervention. However, they should report their concerns and let others get on with doing their jobs. If schools do not draw the boundary, then they will become distracted from their main purpose of learning. This will ultimately affect all the children in the school, including those at most risk.

## FIRST THINGS FIRST

Creating a vision and raising self-esteem are important steps towards achievement of goals. Turning them into reality requires both clarity about purpose (the 'big picture') and attention to the detail of how thousands of interactions – in classrooms and outside them – will lead to the achievement of the vision. Everyone connected with the school needs to know that it is first and foremost a learning community, and that effort will be directed towards ensuring that its learning objectives are achieved.

Learning needs to be at the centre of the school development plan (SDP). Appendix 3 gives an example of how an SDP can be created that starts with this central purpose. It then shows how the school can go about achieving this on a daily basis. It is only when the thousands of daily interactions between adults and children in the school, mainly but not exclusively in the classroom, are all focused on learning that the school will be able to chart its progress.

## EVERYONE A LEARNER

It is essential that all adults in the school are themselves involved in learning. Struggling with a new language or studying for a higher degree are both very good ways of reminding staff of the difficulties of learning. This acts as a reminder that children do not necessarily choose to find something difficult to learn! It also acts as a positive role model for the children – if the teacher and other adults feel the need to learn continuously, this helps make the point that learning is something for everyone and that education is not just a little jug of knowledge waiting to be poured into fairly empty heads.

One thing that is very noticeable when one tries to learn something new as an adult is that everyone has different learning styles. Some like to immerse themselves in a new topic for possibly days, while others like to have short but frequent bursts of activity. The way in which school timetables are organized, both in primary and, more particularly, in secondary schools favours one type of learning style. While it is unlikely that radical changes to this will occur overnight, at least not until we see the full impact of the new ICT technologies, it is worth trying to ensure that a mixture of approaches is used. This maximizes the chances of everyone finding at least something resembling their own natural learning style.

It should also be remembered that people managed to learn important things for millennia without being able to read and write. Children who can read and write find it relatively easy to learn in today's culture. However, it is possible to learn through other methods and a good mixture of approaches can be very successful.

## CREATING THE RIGHT ENVIRONMENT

There is a later chapter on managing the school building(s), but it should be mentioned here that every effort must be made to create a physical environment that is conducive to learning and that promotes this central purpose at every opportunity. Noticeboards inside and outside classrooms, regularly updated with bright displays can be very cost-effective. A mixture of professionally produced materials and pupils' work (only their best) brightens up the school and makes all pupils (adults and children alike) more positive about learning.

Well-drawn murals can be very good, but the temptation to allow just anyone to paint them should be resisted. The quality of resources and work on display should be of the highest order. Anything less than this sends out a message that poor work is all right. Displays need to be updated but there needs to be some realism about this. It is easier to ensure that displays in primary schools are updated reasonably regularly, particularly if non-teaching staff help with them. It is sometimes difficult to ensure that displays in secondary schools do not remain fixed forever. Some find that an Open Evening provides a good opportunity for an annual 'makeover' of all displays, with individual subject areas updating on a smaller scale as they can. The Art department will find that May is a good time to update displays, since many of them use the GCSE coursework as a central part of their promotion of Art. On the other hand, this would not be an appropriate time for Modern Languages staff to update their display work, since much of it has to be covered or removed if examinations are taking place in the classrooms.

Staff who do not update display work, both inside and outside the teaching areas, miss a great chance to reinforce learning. If pupils see lists of key words in various subjects or pictures of the working of a modern computer network when they idly look around the classroom, learning is being reinforced. The other point to be made is that staff whose learning areas do not look professional and positive may well be sending out a subliminal message to the pupils that their class or their subject is not as important as other classes or other subjects.

Pupils are very often more than willing to take responsibility for helping with display work. If they do, they need to be briefed about the importance of high quality. Health and safety issues also need to be addressed – they should not be standing on chairs, if this could lead to them falling off and injuring themselves.

## TEACHING OR LEARNING?

The emphasis of the inspection system that was set up in the 1990s was on the quality of teaching. There is little doubt that the quality of teaching does matter. However, the vast majority of those who operate under the name of 'teacher' in schools are more than capable of teaching, given certain conditions. Experience suggests that attitude, enthusiasm, determination and belief are the key elements of good and great teachers. The observation of teachers during possibly one or two lessons in a certain week does not give much relevant information about their effectiveness in promoting learning. Some very good teachers do not 'shine' during inspections, while some fairly ordinary teachers can 'turn it on' for inspectors (and for team leaders, as part of the performance management process).

Every school needs good and great teachers. If the environment is right – which means dealing with self-esteem and other key points – then teachers can realize their potential. However, it is unhelpful to think that great teaching always leads to great learning. A highly entertaining and popular teacher may actually on occasion hinder learning, if the objectives of lessons have not been planned. If we measure effective teaching by the learning outcomes of the pupils, then it becomes clear that a lot of the most effective learning takes place with good, but not outstanding, teachers. This leads to the hypothesis that the important questions for every headteacher in the area of teaching and learning are:

- ❑ Where is effective learning taking place in this school?
- ❑ How do we create the right conditions for this to happen throughout the school?
- ❑ How can we best use the talents of all our teachers?
- ❑ What do we all need to learn in order to improve learning outcomes?
- ❑ How can we share best practice?

## WHAT ARE THE OUTCOMES?

There are two kinds of outcome resulting from learning – the intended and the unintended. Among the intended should be very specific outcomes (for example, to be able to multiply and divide numbers, be able to spell certain words, be able to remember a periodic table) and more general ones (to be able to work effectively with others, be able to empathize with others). Although the latter outcomes are more difficult to assess, they are probably more important than some of the others.

Unintended outcomes are more interesting. By definition, they have not been planned. In many cases, they will be totally unexpected. This is where the professionalism of teachers needs to be used. A good teacher knows the intended outcomes and builds in some spare time to allow for the unintended to be dealt with. The intended outcomes for a specific lesson may be abandoned on account of an interesting idea that comes up; the overall plan for that class will not, however, be affected, since the teacher will know that the time lost can be made up in a later lesson. It is also important to remember that just because something has been listed as having been taught does not mean that it has been learned!

## MEASURING SUCCESS

There is currently an unhealthy obsession with measuring school success and failure. Indeed, one might sometimes think that the obsession is with failure. The problem is that for every measure of success, there is always a 'But. . .' to be attached. If, for example, a class does well in its Key Stage 1 SATs, what happens if it only does all right at the end of Key Stage 2?

Oranges do not taste nicer because they have been measured, weighed and photographed. They taste nicer if the conditions under which they are grown are right. This is the same for learning. If the conditions are right and good resources are made available, then children learn better. Some form of testing may be used to indicate that this has happened, but the tests themselves contribute very little to the actual learning process. Our society needs to decide at some point when they are going to allow children and schools to flourish. It was in the nineteenth century that the simple truth emerged that if required to do so (by an oppressive regime) teachers will teach to tests. The only things that will be taught will be those that are easily measurable. Maybe a few history lessons – with measurable outcomes – are needed for those who lead education! However, the temptation will have to be resisted to over-test them, lest we impair their willingness to learn!

### What matters to the school?

Schools should measure what is important to them, starting from their stated aims and using whatever methods are appropriate in each case. External examinations will give one measure of progress, while the school needs to look to itself for ways of measuring progress in other areas. The important thing is that one uses information to guide future practice, not as a stick with which to beat people. Schools have lots of information about pupils already. This should be used by teachers and others to improve on previous practice and to ensure that each child has a set of positive learning experiences from the school.

If an intended outcome is to be measured, then it needs to be agreed in advance what it is to be. It will then be easier to work out ways in which the measuring can be done, in a way that actually makes sense. Things such as pupil behaviour need to start with an idea of what the ideal outcome is. Ways of measuring improvements can be agreed – it might involve using an external consultant working to the agenda agreed with the school – and then a conscious effort can be made to start the improvement process. Any external consultant should be someone who has the confidence of the school and who will report dispassionately on their findings after an agreed period of time. If a lot of progress has been made, this will be a cause for celebration. If not, then the whole issue will need to be looked at again. It is vital that all involved share a common purpose of improving all the time by learning all the time.

## COMMUNICATING WITH THE CUSTOMER

The main customers as far as a school is concerned are the pupils and the parents. The school prospectus and any further curriculum details that the school sends out are important ways in which the focus on learning can be communicated and reinforced. A policy on learning, which tries to make sense of the whole range of tools to be used, is very important.

If the school sets out clearly what it hopes to achieve (the acquisition of knowledge, skills and attitudes), how it hopes to do so (through the creation of good learning opportunities inside and outside the classroom) and how parents can help (including details of homework practice), it is well on its way to success. It is also communicating what it feels it should be measured by. The alternative is that school policy is set in response to calls from (sometimes neurotic) parents, whose views may not represent those of most parents.

## PROGRAMMES OF STUDY

A vital part of the school's plan for curriculum delivery is to be found in the programmes of study. While this may be the responsibility of a class teacher in a primary school or of one person for a subject such as Music in a small secondary school, in larger secondary schools there will be more than one teacher responsible for the delivery of subjects such as English, Mathematics, Science, and so on.

In the primary school it is important that a programme of study follows on from what has been previously studied. In the secondary school this is equally important, but the question of comparability for pupils of the same age with different teachers also arises. (This also happens in some large primary schools.) Programmes of study need to set out clearly what every child will be able to do by the end of the year, with details of how differentiation and progression will be managed.

There is a limit on the amount of time teachers have to plan work. There is therefore likely to be a compromise between the desirable and the achievable. All teachers need to have a medium-term plan – for, say five to seven weeks – and more detail for individual lessons. The level of detail required in some schools does appear to be unnecessary and is not legally required. If one does not get some kind of balance in this area, the teachers will become worn out and will not be there to do the teaching.

It is a vital part of the headteacher's role to help staff get this very important balance right. It often requires the courage to stand up to advisers and inspectors, but it goes with the job. It is not an optional extra. Only the headteacher knows exactly what the conditions are like in a particular school and is in the position to defend people who are often trying to do a very difficult job with one hand tied behind their back. There is a difference between setting high ambitions and working hard to achieve them on one hand, and slavishly following the diktats of non-experts on the other.

For GCSE and A level pupils, at least, it can be useful to give out copies of the syllabus before the course starts. They can then see how the teacher is planning the way through the course and can be more involved in ensuring that there is time to get everything done. They are being given the tools for learning anything in the future. If they decide at some time that they would like to study a new subject, they will know how to go about doing so.

## Record-keeping and marking work

Many schools have devised elaborate systems for keeping records of what has been taught. It is difficult to see the point of some of these. The teacher needs to know what the class covered yesterday or last lesson, so that progress is made from one day or week to the next. The headteacher needs to know that there is a programme of work and that it is being followed. Neither of these explicitly requires a lot of detail.

The record of what the individual child has learned is available in books, projects, on the computer network, and so on. If the parent wants to see this, it is not a difficult task to arrange. The other way of finding out what the child knows is to ask them to explain something about, say, early settlements in England.

If an advisor or inspector wishes to check what has been taught, the same kinds of tools are available. Dentists keep a brief record of work carried out on teeth, but the real evidence is visible in the patient's mouth. Schools need to adopt a more realistic sense of record-keeping, thinking more carefully about audience and purpose.

There is little doubt that marking pupils' work is important. If it is not marked, then the pupil will think it doesn't matter and will stop trying. However, there is not much evidence to suggest that spending a long time marking each pupil's work in detail is very productive. It is certainly not cost-effective, when the opportunity cost of spending more time marking is that less time is available for preparing stimulating lessons. Schools can help by encouraging teachers to set at least some tasks, both in class and as homework, which can be self-marked or marked by a companion in the class. A key point here is that pupils are more likely to do this properly if they realize that cheating only stops them learning. This takes time to achieve, but it is far from impossible to do.

## THE TOOLS FOR THE JOB

There has never been a better time to be involved in the business of learning. Lifelong learning is seen as important by society. There is also, at the same time, a great array of learning resources upon which teachers can call. It is worth looking at some of these.

### Books

The days when one, very plain textbook was the only resource available to most pupils and their teachers have gone. There are some very attractive and well-designed books in the market place. The use of colour, clear text, diagrams and pictures means that it is easier to learn than it was in the past. Such books are also much cheaper in real terms than they used to be.

Schools are often asked to recommend reading or study materials. It is worth giving some thought to this beforehand, so that some information can be provided. In the urban school, one has to be careful not to put pressure (even unintended) on parents to buy extra books. In many cases, they will not be able to afford to buy these and their children may then feel under pressure in school for not having them. There is a great market for revision guides, for SATs, GCSE and so on. While some of these will not do much harm, their quality is very variable. It might be worth asking relevant staff to have a look at what is available in bookshops, so that parents can be advised on what to buy, if they really want to do so. Some schools find that the best of them can be useful with classes.

It is important that urban schools try to set aside a good amount of money for books, even in these days of television, computers, and so on. It also needs to be remembered that even books that have been looked after carefully do eventually need to be replaced. Many homes have every gadget imaginable, but few if any books. A large number of adults never read a book – ever. They may read newspapers and magazines, but it is useful to assume that children may not see any books at home and plan accordingly. There can be a real dilemma about whether to allow pupils to take books home, particularly if they may not bring them for the next day's lessons. One way round this is to have a book for home use and different books for school use. This may seem wasteful but even if a book costs £10, that is only £300 for an extra set for a class of 30. Two days' supply cover would pay for that!

### CDs, CD ROMs, cassettes and videos

Most children, even from deprived backgrounds, have access to a CD and/ or cassette player, a television and a video-recorder. Not all this access will be under ideal conditions, of course, but at least the physical tools are likely to be there.

Nowadays, it is relatively cheap to produce CDs on a basic computer. Schools are beginning to realize that they can produce CDs that can include such things as exercises in one or more Modern Foreign Languages. Some of these exercises can be practice or revision, while others can be designated as homework.

There are also many commercially available products. As with books, some are very good and some are a waste of time and money. Again, teachers are in a good position to look at what is available and to recommend them for purchase, either by school or by parents who ask for advice.

## ICT LEARNING RESOURCES

There has been a substantial, but limited, investment of public money in developing ICT resources in schools. Many schools now have computer networks, with the potential for learning that these bring. Headteachers need to encourage the development of teaching methodologies that take account of the vast potential of ICT. However, this needs to be balanced with a realistic assessment of what is feasible in the average school. This depends not only on the availability of technology, but also on the teachers having the knowledge of what is possible. It is no good having the latest hardware and software if those responsible for planning and delivering learning in the school – the teachers – do not know what is available to support their schemes of work and are not confident in including ICT as part of their teaching toolkit.

A useful point for teachers to remember is that they do not have to see the pupils using ICT for it to be effective. Setting challenging work to be completed outside lesson times – either at home or in school (remembering that not all pupils have access to ICT facilities at home) – can be a very cost-effective way of incorporating ICT into programmes of work.

ICT can assist learning in ways that we only understand dimly at present. With continued development and the willing participation of teachers the total learning experience will be transformed.

## Cost-effective solutions

If we want to develop cost-effective learning solutions we need to be clear about what it is we are trying to achieve. As stated already, schools need to focus more sharply on intended learning outcomes than they have in the past. The value of setting out learning outcomes as a measure of progress is that the needs of individual pupils – on which any measure of school progress depends – are put centre stage. Merely recording what has been taught to a class does not tell us what pupils have achieved during a particular series of lessons. This is as true for those who are present in class as it is for those who are not.

Many schools are very keen to use the potential of the Internet in lessons. While it is true that this particular technology has a lot to offer, it can equally send pupils down some very unproductive lanes and learning dead-ends. A school network, with a variety of learning resources available on it, should form the backbone of any e-learning solution. This is likely to provide more reliable access to learning resources, in a more focused form and with more control over the learning environment. Broadband technology can bring the whole Internet into the classroom – and is particularly useful for video-conferencing and sharing teaching/learning expertise – but it is not essential that all pupils can access it at all times.

Some visions of the pupil of the future picture a child with some kind of hybrid telephone/personal digital assistant/laptop computer, with possibly a headset to 'see' what is going on. This sounds more like a nightmare than a desirable vision of the future. The tools of learning that exist today and those that are currently being developed can potentially make learning more effective and more enjoyable. However, schools are not just factories in which young people have a requisite amount of 'knowledge' poured into their heads. The idea of learning must go beyond the mechanistic.

## Theory into practice

The school needs to first of all set a vision for e-learning. All staff need to be involved to varying degrees in this process. Whole-school aims need to be established, dealing with the 'what' and the 'how' of learning. This then needs to be addressed in individual schemes of work, thus ensuring that the overall school vision starts to happen in individual learning situations (usually teachers with pupils in classrooms).

A key to the development of e-learning across the school comes from the sharing of good practice. INSET days offer very cost-effective ways of sharing expertise developed in many classrooms. There is a lot of good experience in every school, just waiting to be shared for the benefit of all. Sometimes staff are diffident about giving the impression that they are role models for everyone else. If it becomes the norm to share some ideas across the school, then this diffidence can be overcome. Pupils can also be asked to identify good practice. They see the teaching across the school in a way that no one else ever does.

## Entitlement

The issue of pupil entitlement arises in every area of the school, but it is particularly important that it is addressed within the area of ICT. This is because, while teachers who are experts in the subject matter may teach some of the ICT curriculum, the use of ICT for learning across the curriculum has to involve all staff. Not all staff are comfortable with ICT tools, but it is essential that this does not lead to some pupils missing out substantially on what should be a basic entitlement. Here are some guidelines for addressing the role of ICT in learning in a staff meeting:

- Involve all staff in deciding what the learning outcomes should be for all pupils. A question such as, 'What would we like each Year 2 or Year 7 pupil to achieve in five years' time?', could be a good starting point.

- ❑ Try to avoid the 'how' too early on or one may end up talking about computers.
- ❑ Use the outcomes of the session to produce some e-learning aims for the school.
- ❑ Ask individual class or subject leaders to translate these into practical activities with their year group or subject area.
- ❑ Evaluate and discuss progress.
- ❑ Share good practice.

## Use of Web sites and e-mail

There is much untapped potential in using Web sites for learning. Resources for learning are beginning to become available to schools, particularly through broadband regional consortia. There are also a lot of learning sites and, particularly, revision sites for examinations such as GCSE. The BBC Web site (www.bbc.co.uk/learning) is a good starting point for those wishing to see what kind of thing is possible.

It is also possible to use e-mail and/or mobile telephone messaging to help pupils with learning, particularly with revision. Some secondary schools are allowing some pupils to e-mail homework queries to teachers; in other cases, staff give out their e-mail address to their classes. This needs to be carefully managed, since it can be a very time-consuming exercise, but there is certainly potential here for the future.

## Interactive whiteboards and other 'future' technologies

As the use of networked learning resources, allied to interactive whiteboards, becomes more prevalent in schools, there will be enormous implications. Headteachers will need to keep themselves informed of developments, so that they can ensure that the school looks clearly and positively at the ways in which learning will change.

For example, lessons will be put on the school network, assembled by teams of teachers and usable by all of them. There will then be the opportunity for pupils who are absent to access these lessons. The question will then inevitably arise: 'If sick pupils can do this themselves – possibly from home as well – why cannot all pupils do likewise?' This is not the place to investigate this, but it is something of which headteachers in particular need to be very aware. A useful INSET activity might focus around the role of ICT in learning and what the classroom of the future (that is, two or three years' time!) might look like.

# SUPPORT FOR LEARNING

Many children in urban schools lack proper facilities and help at home. The unfortunate thing about this is that for those children, a good education may be their only hope for the future. They need more facilities and support than they have at home. Schools in urban areas are often the best – or only – places for these facilities and support to be provided

Examples of what schools are attempting to do include family learning programmes, involving parents of quite young children in learning themselves and in helping their children to learn in turn. Breakfast clubs provide some children with their only opportunity to have something to eat before starting a hard day's work. In some cases, schools are open as early as 8.00 am. Pupils can combine having something to eat with extra literacy lessons, the opportunity to use the school computers and/or library books and perhaps the chance to discuss their progress with a learning mentor.

After-school learning activities are burgeoning in many schools. Study support, with teachers and others paid to help, is proving to be a very effective way of helping children achieve their goals.

7

# GETTING THINGS ORGANIZED

Leaders of schools need to ensure that things run efficiently and effectively. There is not much point in having everyone united behind a vision, with a clear agreement and understanding of purpose, if the organization of the school is a shambles. There is enough evidence to suggest that headteachers who are *effective* visionaries are either those who are good at organizing things themselves or those who ensure that someone else with good organizational skills manages the process.

## ORGANIZING ONESELF

The first few weeks of headship are often like the calm before the storm. Suddenly one carries the ultimate responsibility, which is not the same as being part of a senior management team. There is no set of rules about how one should organize one's time. Should one have a teaching commitment? It is the headteacher's call. Should one have regular meetings every morning with the business manager? It is the headteacher's call. Should one keep one's office door open, closed or ajar? It is the headteacher's call.

What is unusual during the first few weeks is that there may well be nothing that the new headteacher actually *has* to do. Schools are usually very good at running themselves in the short term and this is what can happen at this time. Everyone is waiting to see how things will change. Some will decide that this is their big opportunity to get extra non-teaching time, to ask for promotion, to try to get rid of some of their responsibilities, in general to impress. Others – probably the majority – will get on with their own work. The bit that can seem alarming to start with is that from day one the headteacher is responsible for everything – including any disasters – but they may not be doing anything yet that contributes directly to the work of the school.

## PRIORITIZING

After the first few weeks, the headteacher is likely to find that there will be a lot of demands on their time. This is where some decisions have to be made about priorities. Some questions to ponder:

- What are the most important things I should do? (It may be useful to list these in writing.)
- What am I spending most of my time on? Does this time allocation equate to the priorities identified under the first question?
- How much time should I give to the pupils? Who should sort out disciplinary matters? (The general answer to the latter question may be that the headteacher should not be directly involved in day-to-day discipline. However, in the early stages it may be sensible – or possibly necessary – to establish clear parameters of behaviour. This may require a more direct involvement in pastoral matters, at least for a specific period of time.)
- Should I have a teaching commitment? The advantage of teaching is that it enables the headteacher to learn about some of the pupils. Some feel that it also establishes their credibility with teaching staff, although it is not necessarily the best way of doing this. The disadvantage is that there may be times when the headteacher needs to go to an important meeting and has to leave the class with someone else. At least if there is no teaching commitment, there can be no complaints about lateness to lessons or other staff having to cover the headteacher's classes at short notice. It is worth noting that inspectors will observe the headteacher teaching on the same basis as everyone else, so if a commitment is made then it needs to be taken seriously.
- Will I be available to parents on an ad hoc basis, on an appointment basis, or only when other channels have been explored? Will I ask for parents to be put through to me if I am free or will I apply some form of filtering to calls? (Most calls from reasonable parents are to do with some concern about their child. In most cases, this is best dealt with by a member of the pastoral staff and parents understand this. Once the headteacher is clear that procedures are in place for parental concerns to be dealt with quickly and effectively, then the need for parents to speak directly to the headteacher will be lessened.)

The role of the headteacher with regard to the community also needs to be considered. More will be said about this in a later chapter, but certainly the matter needs to be given specific attention. This is particularly so in urban schools.

## Dealing with mail and the telephone

Headteachers need to decide how to deal with post (and faxes), including the weekly mail bag from the Local Education Authority (where this happens). Some headteachers open their own mail, while others see this as a waste of time. One difficulty these days of asking the Office staff to open the mail, is that confidential mail is often not highlighted as such, while some mail that is labelled 'private and confidential – to be opened by the addressee only' is just junk mail. Not everyone helpfully posts their junk mail to schools in transparent envelopes that can be dumped straight in the filing cabinet under the desk!

Very often the headteacher is in school before the Office staff and a decision needs to be taken on whether to answer the telephone or not. Usually such calls are about absence, but occasionally they are about something more important. The author's experience is that it does no harm at all to answer the phone at this time of the morning, and that parents are usually very appreciative. Answering the phone during lunchtime is probably less useful, since it is often somebody looking to speak to a teacher and the headteacher is likely to have to pass this on to the administrative staff to deal with.

Incidentally, senior staff who need to contact parents often find that ringing them from home in the evening can be very effective, provided that they remember to dial 141 first. (This means that the teacher's home telephone number does not become quickly available to most of the parents within two hours!)

# TIME MANAGEMENT

There are many and varied courses, books and theories about how to manage one's time effectively. They all boil down to one simple premise: if a leader does not manage their time, then events will. Some suggestions are made here, but responsibility for everyone's use of their time ultimately falls to the individual. Time is limited and the opportunity cost of using time to do one thing is that other things cannot be done.

The first point to be made is that prioritizing will give some indication of what one should be spending one's time doing. Ways need to be found of ensuring that the really important things – for example, preparing a presentation for an INSET day – do not get rushed because the headteacher has been running around looking at broken windows or picking up litter in the corridors. One of the most important functions of local meetings of headteachers is that it affords the opportunity to talk to others about how they manage their time and how they deal with unproductive demands on their time.

## Regular reviews

One of the paradoxes of time management is that the busier one is, the more important it is to take time out to think about how to manage all the things that appear on one's desk. At least once a year – and perhaps more frequently – the headteacher should sit down and reflect on what they should be doing to improve the effectiveness of the school. Time management is one of those areas where the ultimate solution is never to be found. It is also one of those areas where it is easy to slip into bad habits.

Staff should notice each September that the headteacher has been thinking about time management, by the way in which they use their time. This is a good way of knowing that the thinking is working. It is important for the good of the school that the headteacher does manage time effectively and that others are encouraged to do so as well. If the headteacher works with other members of the senior management team so that they realize the importance of effective time management, then they are in a better position to help others to do the same.

## Diaries and planners

For a classroom teacher, the school timetable creates the structure of the day. For the headteacher, this is not the case. Some kind of diary or planner is therefore essential. This applies to most members of the senior management team, but even a deputy headteacher may find that a simple diary will suffice. The headteacher, on the other hand, needs a fairly sophisticated diary system. It is also important to decide right at the beginning whether the headteacher is the only person to make appointments in the diary or whether one or more of the administrative staff will be allowed to do so.

Traditional paper diaries come in several formats. A small pocket diary is easy to carry round, while an A4-size diary allows more detail to be written and may also be used to record the outcomes of meetings. Many use an A5-size diary as a compromise. It can be carried in a briefcase or handbag, but is still large enough to allow detailed notes to be written. Security is important, since no back-up exists for paper diaries.

A variation on this theme is to use a paper organizer or 'Filofax'. These are not as popular as they once were, but they still have their adherents. One of the advantages of this type of organizer is that key data, such as contact details, can be carried forward from year to year. There is also quite a sophisticated range of additional inserts available, such as a calculator, ruled and unruled note pages, and so on.

## Electronic organizers

While many headteachers still use paper-based diary systems, more and more are switching to electronic versions. There are three kinds of electronic organizer available that are relevant to the leader of a school. Very small databanks are not really much use for running a school!

The first main option is a handheld computer with a (small) keyboard. The main selling point of this type of handheld computer is its keyboard, which is convenient for entering data such as telephone numbers, appointments or notes. Having small fingers can be a help! It does not usually come with Windows applications (of which more later) but can usually be set up to swap and/or synchronize information with a laptop or desktop computer.

The second option is to buy what is often referred to as a 'palmtop', of which the manufacturer Palm probably sells the most. However, there are also other models available. One should look at several and try them out before deciding which one suits best. Many people consider it worth paying extra to have a colour screen as opposed to a monochrome one. The main disadvantage of a colour screen, apart from the extra cost, is that it is very demanding on battery life. However, it can be kept plugged in while on the headteacher's desk and it is definitely much easier to read than a black and white screen. Although palmtops usually have their own software, there are easy links with laptops and desktops, for backing up data and sharing it with your main computer. In place of a keyboard, data is usually entered via a stylus. Some users like the handwriting software that comes with these and find that they can get the computer to recognize their 'scrawl' to an acceptable degree. There is also the option of having a small 'keyboard' on screen, which one taps with a stylus (a blunt biro!).

The third option is to buy a palmtop with a special form of Windows software. This will usually have cut-down versions of such applications as Word, Excel and so on. Links with the full version of these applications are quite easy to achieve.

The two main advantages of a handheld/palmtop computer over a paper-based one are the ability to organize and search data on the one hand, and the security of being able to back up data.

A modern electronic handheld computer is a very sophisticated piece of kit. It offers many useful facilities for a headteacher, to help manage time effectively. It will have a diary/calendar function, allowing appointments to be entered, with a time slot for each. If the appointment is subsequently changed, the date and/or time can easily be amended and it then appears in its own slot. There is also provision with each appointment to add notes. This can be useful if one attends a meeting and wishes to keep some information for future use. Reminders can be set for minutes, hours and even days in advance.

These computers also offer the facility to keep lists of contacts. A huge range of data can be entered for any contact, from name, address and telephone numbers of the contact to details of their wedding anniversary, birthday, details of their spouse, children and so on.

Tasks can be set, with daily reminders popping up if required, and notes can be made as freestanding items. The functions already noted can make a great difference to the life of a busy headteacher. A small handheld computer that has pocket versions of Word, Excel and Money allows files to be easily transferred from a main computer or full-size laptop computer.

Other functions, which may actually not save time, include video-clip viewers, music players, and electronic books. The Internet and e-mail can also be accessed using a handheld computer and a compatible mobile telephone. There are also some models available that include a built-in mobile telephone, thus obviating the need for a separate telephone.

A key point about using a pocket computer is that it can be set up to synchronize with a desktop or laptop computer. The computer can be set to provide a reminder to do this on a daily or weekly basis. Once the data is on a larger computer, it can then be printed off in a variety of formats. It can also be made available to other staff in the school, via the computer network.

## Senior staff duty

Many schools use a 'senior staff duty' system to allow members of the senior management team to have periods of time when they will be undisturbed by day-to-day matters. When something urgent arises, the administrative staff know who to turn to. If the headteacher decides to be part of this system, then it is important that a realistic amount of time is allocated and then, as far as possible, that it is adhered to. Some headteachers do not take part in such a system, but instead make themselves available at suitable times. Some schools have one senior deputy headteacher who carries out most of these duties, with some backup when they are teaching; in this case, they are likely to have a substantially reduced teaching load. It is important to ensure that all members of the system understand its rationale and can see that it is fair.

One way in which a headteacher can get to know a lot of pupils is by taking a turn at doing dinner duty. It is worth considering having set days for dinner duty – which can then be rearranged if necessary – rather than the headteacher doing dinner duty every day. Once or twice a week can be useful, but it is difficult to see how the headteacher doing dinner duty every day of the week is the most effective use of their time.

### Keeping in touch

The headteacher of the modern urban school is unlikely to be found residing in the school all the time. There are meetings to attend, opportunities to research, personal development to undertake, which all take the headteacher away from the school. Indeed, in some schools it is possible for the headteacher to be on site, without anyone knowing precisely where they are.

Nearly every headteacher now has at least one mobile telephone, sometimes supplemented with a pager. It is possible to be in contact 24/7, as the saying goes. How far is this desirable? Ground rules need to be clearly established about when, and by whom, the headteacher should be contacted when they are out of school. In a well-run school, this might happen only once a month or even less frequently. In a school where the headteacher is not too confident in the ability of the staff to manage, this may happen very frequently indeed. The ultimate aim of every headteacher should be that the telephone never rings, but sometimes a less than perfect situation does exist. It needs to be clear who will ring and in what circumstances. Allowing individuals to decide what is important means that the headteacher may be contacted by a diligent head of department who wants a decision on buying a new filing cabinet – after all, it may be very important to them! – while a major disaster like a flood in the boiler room may not be seen as needing a call to be made.

If time is money, and the opportunity cost of doing one thing is not being able to do another, then everyone needs to know what is important and what is not. They are more likely to be able to do so if there is effective delegation.

## DELEGATING EFFECTIVELY

There are three key parts to effective delegation. Firstly, the limits and responsibilities of delegation must be clear, both to the person delegating the task and also to the person who is taking it on. A good example might be staff development. Let us suppose that the headteacher has decided to delegate this to an assistant headteacher. The limits of delegation might be budgetary (only refer back if the budget is in danger of going over or if an individual's share is more than a certain amount) or it might be that certain courses (say, award-bearing ones and/or those lasting more than two days) require consultation with the headteacher. Issues to be agreed are whether the school pays the full costs of award-bearing courses (such as higher degrees) and whether courses must be very directly linked to the member of staff's specific responsibilities. (There are two reasons why one should be generous with regard to the latter: firstly, it is good for all staff to be undertaking further study, as this enhances the view that the school is a learning community for all stages in life; secondly, courses such as counselling can be very useful for non-teaching staff, since the latter are often an informal – and trusted – source of advice for pupils.) It is good practice to try to ensure that senior staff have some responsibility for a budget. This may be the budget for a particular initiative (for example, one or more areas of the Excellence in Cities initiative) or for a particular area of school activity (for example, capitation).

The second key point about delegation is that the headteacher must let the member of staff get on with it. This works both ways. While in the early stages one might expect some referral back to the headteacher, if this persists then the decision to delegate is called into question. The member of staff must, however, always feel relaxed about discussing a delegated matter with the headteacher. Sometimes a sounding board is all that is being sought.

Thirdly, tasks must be delegated to those who can carry them out, or who have the potential to do so. If it is not clear that someone has the ability to carry out a delegated task effectively, consideration could be given to delegating it for a short period of time. If the member of staff is not up to this particular job – which does not necessarily mean that they are incapable of doing other things – then the task can be withdrawn without it looking like a demoralizing vote of no confidence.

## Do unto others. . .

The practice of effective delegation should be encouraged throughout the school. Deputy and assistant headteachers can set an example for the rest of the staff by following the headteacher's example. The question every manager should always ask is, 'Could someone else with other qualifications do this job, and possibly more effectively?' There is a wide range of jobs that can be done very well by others, particularly those requiring good administrative skills. Well-trained administrative staff have the potential to vastly improve the ways in which schools are run.

### Preparing other staff for headship

Helping staff prepare themselves for promotion outside the school is an important part of the headteacher's job. In some cases the school will have one or more deputy headteachers who are hoping to apply for a headship at some point in the future. If this is the case, consideration should be given to giving opportunities to undertake at least part of the jobs that the headteacher has decided are not going to be delegated. For example, in many schools the planning of the overall school budget is done by the headteacher, sometimes in conjunction with the business manager. In some schools, this is delegated to a deputy headteacher, while in others the responsibility is shared between one or more members of the senior management team.

## USE OF ICT TO IMPROVE SCHOOL EFFECTIVENESS

Accurate information is as an essential aid to good management. Nowadays, this means having a good computerized management information system (MIS). Many schools, primary and secondary, have networks that extend beyond the school office and allow for the input and use of data by a wide range of staff.

### Information

Schools need to be clear about the kind of information they wish to store on a computerized system. In general, the more information that can be kept in this way, the more likely it is that it can be shared. Once it can be shared, then the school can be better managed. The key to this is 'definition' – what kind of information do we want, how will we get it (and keep it up to date), how will we use it and who will have access to it?

There are very many kinds of information that it can be useful to have about pupils, staff and physical resources. There are pieces of general, non-academic information about pupils that it is important for schools to have. This will include names, date of birth, address, postcode, telephone number (including emergency contact numbers) and so on. Schools also store a lot of assessment data and increasingly this is done at pupil level. Such data can be used to discuss progress with pupils. It is also used to aggregate and compare the achievement levels of pupils in different subjects, by gender, by ethnic background, by socio-economic grouping (using, for example, entitlement to free school meals as an indicator), and so on.

Detailed records of pupils' special needs, including information relating to whether they are on the Special Educational Needs (SEN) register, can also be kept. Software packages are continually being developed, both as separate programmes and as options within a larger package, which make the process of data collection in this area much easier to manage.

The kind of data that schools may wish to gather on a computer about staff includes full names (and possibly previous names), preferred title (for example, Mr, Ms, Miss, Mrs), address, telephone number (and whether it is ex-directory or not), e-mail address, name of next of kin, emergency contacts (including telephone numbers and relationship to the member of staff), length of service in the school, qualifications, salary point, DfES reference number, employee reference number, responsibility within the school (for example, assistant teacher of English, head of Science, deputy headteacher, marketing manager), ethnic group and/or religion and nationality. It is also useful to include a record of in-service training, subjects taught, other subjects qualified to teach (including level), membership of professional organizations (for example, subject association or a management institute) and extra-curricular interests and aptitudes. Performance management information can also be organized and stored effectively in this way.

It is possible to store very useful data relating to school buildings, including capital spending, routine repairs and maintenance, the cost of utilities and resources for learning. This makes the job of managing much easier, ensuring that members of the senior management team and governors, in particular, have the right information on which to base key strategic management decisions.

The need for up-to-date and accurate information about finance is paramount. Now that school budgets amount to millions of pounds each year they need to be able to project spending, model it and monitor it. Even before budgets are known, senior managers in schools should be projecting costs for the next financial year and beyond. Different 'models' can show what will happen with a variety of funding possibilities. Variables can be changed and the effect on the total budget is then more easily seen. Monitoring the budget is also vital and a good MIS allows for this. It is possible to 'profile' spending for such items as salaries (changes often occur in September and at other times during the year) and for utilities such as gas and electricity. With many years of experience, schools are now much better at dealing with this type of budgetary fluctuation.

## Improving data collection

Schools are increasingly recognizing that they spend a lot of time entering information into their MIS, which probably exists on one or more computers somewhere else. Some examples may be useful to illustrate this. There is a lot of data stored about individual children before they register for their first school. If this data can be sent electronically to the child's school, this will save a lot of valuable clerical time. While there may be difficulties in getting this information electronically about four- or five-year-olds, once the child is in the school system, it is wasteful for the kind of details mentioned above to be typed out manually every year and, in particular, when the child transfers to another school.

## Improving data management

It is very important that schools take a strategic view of information gathering and, vitally, information use. It is pointless spending thousands of pounds on hardware, software and staff time to collect information, which is then not fully used.

Schools might find it useful to have a brainstorming session, involving representatives of teaching and non-teaching staff, to audit the present information and how it is used. The group could suggest ways of improving data management and ways in which it could be better used. A good approach would be to ask, 'What data do we collect?', 'How do we collect it?', 'What do we do with it?' and 'What would happen if we stopped collecting it?' The answers to these questions will help to focus the mind very clearly on key management issues.

## Is it cost-effective?

When buying computer systems, it is important to consider the total cost of purchase. It is easy to make the mistake of buying cheap 'boxes' and then not noticing the additional costs that can accrue for maintenance and replacement. It is also easy to forget about the staffing costs in using software. Good software may be more expensive to start with, but the saving in staff costs can often make the best software the cheapest in the medium and long term. Staff costs include training (good software will need less training and will be easier to learn), time entering data into a system (can be less if the software is user-friendly) and time spent on 'interrogating' the data (it can sometimes take a long time to get the information one wants from the system).

Staff time responding to requests for data can be time-consuming. Since the government launched its own Information Management Strategy (IMS), matters have improved for schools. The DfES worked with major software suppliers to ensure that there is a common basic data set of information (basically, an agreement on the data that is needed by the school and by others) and that major pieces of software to be used in the schools are interoperable (that is, they will work with each other). Even so, headteachers need to be aware that there are lots of people wanting data from schools, for research and so on. Schools need to remember that time is money and be judicious in their use of staff time in responding to such requests.

## Parent access to school information

It is possible to allow parents to access key information about their children across the Internet. This can include general information about the school (much like exists on a school Web site), but also specific information about their child. The way the system works is that schools decide what information will be available to parents, who are then given a password that allows them access to this information directly from a remotely-managed site. The information is gathered in the school and then uploaded to the host site. If the updating is done on a daily basis, then the information is available very quickly. Parents can log in from home or from work (where they are permitted to do so). Options include the provision of attendance and/or assessment data, information about forthcoming events in the school, details of examinations, the homework that has been set for the night, the classes the child is in and the school timetable.

The headteacher needs to manage the process very carefully. For example, loading attendance data up on a daily basis means that it has to be totally accurate. One way of doing this is to recommend to parents that if their child appears to be absent without their knowledge, they should check this first with the school. However, the school office staff are reliant on the same data, which means that if parents do call the school with a query it may be necessary for someone from the office to physically check if a pupil is present or not.

If homework details are to be included in the information available to parents, then thought needs to be given to the logistics (and time) spent by teachers in putting this data onto the system. If the headteacher decides that this kind of system is worth pursuing, it might be best to start with some data first and then consider extending its use later. It must always be remembered that time spent loading data into a system, is time not available for doing other things. In the case of teachers, this is teaching time, which actually might be more cost-effectively spent with children in the classroom than with a computer. The keen headteacher must consider if parents will use the information and if staff can cope with keeping it up to date.

### E-mail

The use of e-mail, both within the school and beyond, can be a very useful aid for school management. However, a policy needs to be established that covers such things as who is to send e-mails, to whom, for what purposes and within what parameters (it is possible to swamp oneself with e-mail if one is not careful). Care needs to be taken that the use of e-mail does not replace human contact. Many headteachers use e-mail regularly to keep in touch with colleagues, to share ideas and to seek help.

## HOLIDAYS

One of the tests of how well the school is organized lies in the question of the headteacher's holidays. It is important that all staff get a proper break from work if they are to continue to be fresh and innovative. This applies particularly to the headteacher, who needs to be able to be positive in difficult times. In practice, the only way in which many headteachers will get a rest from work is to go away on holiday. Staying at home and just 'popping into school' or being in constant touch by mobile telephone is difficult to operate as a policy.

It is a good idea to allocate members of the senior management team to take responsibility for being on call during holiday times, particularly in the summer months. Like all delegation, it should be clear what is expected (for example, to call into school once or twice a week?) and what needs to be referred to the headteacher.

# 8

# PAYING FOR IT ALL

The school budget is a vital building block in the creation of an effective school. Expenditure should reflect priorities, though this is not always easy to either evaluate or to achieve. Priority number one is to ensure that the budget balances. It is no good having a good ethos, high morale and a clear sense of purpose, if the school cannot pay its way.

It should be noted that the governors must approve the annual school budget, but they can delegate the detailed discussion of it to a committee or to the headteacher. The formal approval must, though, take place at a full meeting of the governors. This section will assume that a lot of the detailed work will be done by the headteacher, possibly in close consultation with the business manager and/or the senior management team.

## SETTING A BUDGET

This detailed work will involve looking ahead at likely expenditure and then trying to match it to the school budget, when it becomes known. One needs to start with planned expenditure first, since this is what the school would like to do. If it turns out that not enough money is available, then cuts will need to be made. If more becomes available, then it is useful to have some further ideal items in mind.

### The annual cycle

Although a school budget operates with effect from April of each year, the process of setting it begins in earnest from the previous September. That is the time to look forward to possible changes in the September of the following year. Changes in pupil numbers may be on the horizon. In the case of the primary school, this information should be available through the Local Education Authority, which will have access to birth and mobility rates. Secondary schools need to know if there are more or fewer numbers in the primary schools from which they draw their pupils.

It may be that the school is thinking of changes to the curriculum, which may have implications for staffing. This in turn will have an impact on the budget. New plans for extension or contraction of the school building may be on the horizon, which will again have implications for the budget.

Since the largest part of any school budget is staffing, and the largest part of the staffing budget is expenditure on teachers, the headteacher needs to sit down with at least the deputy headteacher in charge of curriculum in September, to discuss likely staffing needs for the following academic year. This is despite the fact that the timetable for the current academic year has only started to operate!

## What costs the most?

Every school has a different way of organizing its budget, but the following set of budget headings sets out one way of structuring expenditure. It is not the only way of doing this (for example, a school might wish to include the cost of caretakers under a premises heading), but it allows some key points to be made:

- Staffing, including teachers, supply cover and/or insurance, service level agreements (personnel, finance, etc), administrative staff, technicians, classroom assistants, caretakers, midday supervisors, staff services (employee insurance, staff travel, etc);
- Capitation, including books, furniture, equipment (including computers) and examination costs (in secondary schools);
- Premises, including repairs and maintenance, planned improvements, vandalism and vandalism insurance, fire and security alarms, grounds maintenance, cleaning contract, school meals, gas, electricity, water and sewerage, general rates;
- Miscellaneous, including postage, advertising, telephones, provision for disciplinary exclusions.

## Predicting costs

It is not necessary to start with a blank sheet. The school is currently operating a budget – unless it is being set up for the first time – and the costs of various items will be known. It is good practice to budget for the maximum anticipated expenditure and then shocks do not appear. It is also good practice to set a contingency amount for the unexpected. For example, a burst pipe that leads to the boiler room being flooded over a cold New Year might cost more than £20,000: the school will pay the water company for the unwanted water, the fire brigade to pump it out again, various firms for repairing the leak, replacing the electric cables and boiler attachments that have been damaged, and possibly overtime payments to the caretaker!

## Staffing

This is likely to be the largest item on the school budget. Some businesses spend a fairly small proportion of their budget on staffing, but schools are very labour intensive. In particular the cost of teaching staff will loom very large on the budget.

When working out the cost of staff, it is important to ensure that 'on-costs' (employer contribution to national insurance and pensions) are included. A basic classroom teacher, without allowances but with five years' or so experience, will cost the school in excess of £30,000 per year. Senior staff will cost even more. This is worth bearing in mind when deciding whether to take on an extra teacher, or to allocate more non-teaching time for some administrative duty that could be done by somebody else on a lower salary scale.

One point to note about staffing is the notion of 'incremental drift', whereby teachers (and others) who have not reached the top of an incremental scale will cost more per year, even without promotion. A school with a number of relatively young teachers will find the cost of employing the same number of teachers higher each year. Some of this may be offset by the retirement of older and/or more senior staff, but this does not always happen very conveniently in each school.

There would appear to be a drift in schools, whereby the proportion of the budget spent on teachers is decreasing and that spent on other staff is increasing. This takes account of the increase in the number of support staff, including administrators and teaching assistants. Nevertheless, teachers are still the big budget item.

Ways of saving on staffing include keeping a careful eye on the total number of staff, employing non-teaching staff to do specific tasks that teachers do not need to do, and taking the opportunity of staff leaving to look at other ways of achieving the same end. For example, the school may have more deputy headteachers than other schools of similar size. When one retires, the question of whether that person needs to be replaced by another deputy headteacher needs to be asked.

When seeking to enhance support to teachers, it also needs to be considered whether purchasing some new software for the school network might be more cost-effective than employing an extra administrative officer.

For example, if data is regularly written out by teachers that is then entered into a school network by others, it might be easier if teachers could do this directly themselves. Software that initially looks expensive may turn out to be cheap in the medium term.

## Capitation

Schools still need books but they also need a lot of other resources as well. It is wise to devise some kind of formula for making a basic allocation of money to each budget holder. In the primary school this may be the year teacher or a language coordinator. In the secondary school this is likely to be the heads of department. The advantage of having a clear formula is that every budget holder knows in advance what money is available for running their budget area and what it has to cover. It is important that as much responsibility is devolved to budget holders (in line with the way in which money is now delegated directly to schools), and therefore items such as photocopying, replacement of damaged textbooks, stationery, and so on ought to be part of this basic budget. If they save on, for example, photocopying then that money is available for them to use on buying new books or extra stationery. Additional requests can then be made for further funding. Some useful points are:

- ❑ The money should be for one-off expenditure. (If this is not the case, the headteacher will find the scope for development restricted in later years.)
- ❑ Those asking for extra money should set out clearly what learning gains are likely to result from the granting of the extra money and how it relates to the school development plan.
- ❑ There should be the opportunity to indicate if the expenditure could be phased over more than one year.
- ❑ Any subsequent budgetary demands arising from this should be clearly indicated. (For example, if a new Mathematics course is introduced in Year 7, will there be a need for new books for each of the next four years? If a new set of reading books is introduced in Year 3, will this have a knock-on effect when those children enter Year 4?)

Unfortunately, one of the side effects of success for secondary schools is that examination costs will rise. Schools are not always aware of this, and the senior member of staff who takes responsibility for examination entries needs to be asked annually if there are any large increases expected in expenditure under this heading.

It is nothing short of a national scandal that so much of school budgets have to be spent on examinations, directly (GCSEs) and indirectly (SATs, which are centrally funded but which take money that could be spent in schools). A large amount of it could be spent on far more educationally useful things, such as learning mentors!

## Premises

The upkeep of the premises can use up a substantial part of the school budget. In many schools the state of the premises is such that repairs may amount to little more than putting a 'sticking plaster' over something that really needs a proper overhaul. A good example of this is flat roofs. A flat roof can be a reasonably cost-effective solution for a school, but only if it is properly maintained. There are schools on which sit roofs in the region of 50 years old, which were made to last for 20! The only decent solution for schools in this situation is to try to get the roof replaced.

In the event that some maintenance is necessary, it is wise to get as much done at once as possible. If even a three-year view is taken, it can pay to have one job done costing £5,000, instead of three separate jobs done each year at a total cost of possibly £7,000. The non-monetary costs of stress and internal decoration that arise when roofs leak, are additional reasons why the first option is preferable.

Some schools have found it beneficial to use some of the repairs and maintenance budget to employ an extra caretaker or handyman, on a full- or part-time basis. If the school is eligible for funding for out of hours activities, this may also help with funding this extra caretaking post. Having an extra person on site also allows the school to be occupied for longer periods of time, which may reduce the costs arising from vandalism. (More will be said about this in the next chapter.)

There are two ways of dealing with grounds maintenance. If the school has extensive grounds, then it may be worth employing a gardener. This works well when this person is good and is healthy. It can be a problem if the gardener takes ill for a longish period of time. With a grounds maintenance contract one can specify exactly what is required – for example, 40 cuts of the grass per year, reseeding of football pitch every May, marking out of athletics field for summer sports – and the contractor spreads any risks of staff absence across a larger number of people.

Schools may opt to run their own school meals service, or hand the management of it to an outside contractor. Some urban schools find that large specialist contractors are not interested in taking on their school meals service, particularly if there are a lot of free school meals. Many local education authorities continue to offer a service, while some schools – usually, but not necessarily, larger ones – manage their own service. In the latter case, it is vital to have a really good catering manager.

Many urban schools have large numbers of pupils who are entitled to free school meals. In this case, the local education authority will allocate money to pay for these. However, some local education authorities provide a very small amount of money for a so-called 'set meal'. Schools can choose to allocate more per pupil, but this has to come from the main school budget. Schools are also at liberty to set their own prices. Some use their pricing policy to encourage healthy eating, with sandwiches being subsidized by profits from less healthy options.

School cleaning is similar to school meals provision, in that schools can opt to employ their own staff or use a contractor. It should be noted that any change in the contract is only likely to relate to the management of the contract, since staff are likely to have employment rights in the event of the contract being awarded to someone else. Some primary schools in particular find it beneficial to employ their own cleaners. There are even cases where sixth formers are employed as cleaners, either in their own school or another local one.

Utilities such as gas and electricity can cost quite a lot for a large school. Even for a small school, their cost can use up quite a considerable proportion of the annual budget. It is worth checking if the school is entitled to any discounts for electricity usage. Sometimes this is based not on the amount of electricity consumed in total, but rather on the maximum amount consumed at a peak time. In effect, then, the usage in the evening may not cost any extra at all. It is a good idea to budget for the worst-case scenario of a very cold winter, which might then yield some savings if it turns out to be mild. One should not be risking the school's future on an over-optimistic view of next year's weather!

If a school is due to get new boilers, under a capital scheme, it is worth checking the cost of having gas rather than oil. It is imperative to ensure that new boilers are efficient in the use of fuel and relatively cheap to maintain.

## Miscellaneous expenditure items

Schools can become quite excited about making savings on postage and telephone bills. While it is true that some savings can be made, it is also true that the telephone costs in particular have decreased in real terms in the last decade. Large schools may have seven or more telephone lines – say, three main lines, another one for security, one to link the fire alarm to the local fire brigade, one for a fax machine and one for access to the Internet. There are also likely to be one or more mobile phones, paid for by the school, to keep in touch with key staff (for example, the headteacher) or to give to staff taking pupils on visits away from the school. Many schools have even more lines than this.

It may be worth looking at getting discounts on line rental and considering the bulk purchase of time. Some schools use leased lines, particularly for Internet access. Internal telephone systems can also add to the cost. It is also possible with some broadband connections to get unlimited telephony between schools and/or the local authority, for a fixed annual charge.

Some local authorities can provide detailed advice on all matters to do with the purchase of telephony services and this advice should be actively sought. The situation in this area is changing all the time and the school needs to act on the best advice available at the time it is entering into contracts.

The cost of postage is usually seen as the cost of the stamps. However, there is another hidden cost, which is the staff time needed to get the post together, weigh and stamp it, and then take it to a post box or to the post office. If the school does not have a franking machine, there is also the cost of keeping track of expenditure on stamps. If the school does have a franking machine, only certain staff should know the code that allows it to operate.

Many schools find that the judicious use of a fax machine can reduce the need for posting some items, although many people send a fax, ring to check if it has been received and then put a copy in the post!

If the school sets aside a budget for advertising – in addition to a separate budget for advertising staff vacancies – then it needs to work out what the objectives of this budget are before just agreeing to place advertisements. There is a little (or maybe large) industry out there trying to get schools to advertise in every kind of magazine imaginable. Somebody should be given the job of ensuring that any advertising achieves at least one of the school's aims. This may be a selfish one, such as recruiting extra pupils, or it may be altruistic, such as supporting a local hospital. If someone rings who asks for the headteacher by name and then starts enquiring about their health, there is a good chance it is a sales pitch!

Many schools have decided that all their work for charity, including fund-raising, advertising in booklets and making donations, are under the control of one person or a small committee of senior staff. This means that all requests can be directed easily when they appear in the school office. Large charities operate like this and there is no reason why schools cannot do the same.

## BUDGETARY CONTROL

It is important that all budget holders understand that being responsible for even quite a small budget has implications. The following sets out a short policy, which could be included in a staff handbook:

> The following procedures apply to budget holders and represent practice in line with auditors' recommendations and school policies.
>
> - ❑ Budget holders are entrusted with the spending and monitoring of money allocated. For departmental [class] spending, updates are regularly provided for budget holders to check. Permission to spend over the allocated budget must be obtained in advance from the headteacher.
> - ❑ Orders should normally be placed by using a requisition form, obtainable from the Bursar [school secretary]. They will then be processed and sent on an official order form. Orders may only be made by telephone if they have been specifically agreed with the Bursar [school secretary] in advance and an order number has been obtained. The school is not responsible for payment of goods/services unless their purchase has been properly authorized.
> - ❑ When inspection copies or goods on approval have been received, the invoice must be handed immediately to the Bursar [school secretary]. It will be retained in the Office while the appropriate budget holder makes a decision on whether to retain or return the goods. The school is not responsible for payment of goods/services unless this procedure has been followed.
>
> Register of pecuniary interests:
>
> All members of staff with responsibility for spending school money (ie budget holders) are required to sign the register of pecuniary interests on appointment and at the beginning of each school year. They must indicate if they have any pecuniary interest in a company, organization or individual from which the school may buy goods or services. Nil returns are required.

In larger schools – where more than one person works in the Office – it may be wise to adopt a policy of separation of duties, with one person normally placing orders and another one arranging for invoices to be paid.

There are likely to be local rules governing the purchase of goods and equipment. The headteacher should ensure that these are understood and also that the governors set sensible buying policies. If the local education authority maintains a register of approved contractors, it makes sense for schools to use people from that list. They will have been checked out by the local authority, which saves each school a lot of time and effort. The school should spend its time and effort finding the best contractors on the list and using them. If a contractor approaches a school that is not on the list, they should be encouraged to apply to be included on it. Although voluntary aided schools may not have to use approved contractors, many find that the local authority list is worth using.

With regard to the purchase of large items of equipment, there may be local rules governing the number of tenders needed for purchasing items over a certain value. The governors need to look carefully at these, since in some cases the amounts are unrealistic in the 21st century, after decades of inflation. There are sometimes problems in getting more than one quotation, particularly if a local firm (for example, a building contractor) knows that the school is not likely to use its services.

Another area where there may be difficulties in getting more than one quotation is when the item to be purchased is a proprietary one. This happens often with computers, where the upgrade of the software to run a network may only be available from one firm. Where software licences are to be purchased for, say, Microsoft Office, it can be useful to use the central purchasing unit of the local authority to get price comparisons. Most suppliers of software to schools see the point of matching these, since they will lose the custom otherwise. It is wise to ensure that large items of expenditure are approved by the governors and that the reasons for deviating from the rules on, for example, the number of quotations, are clearly explained in the minutes of the meeting.

The question of virement – moving money from one budget heading to another – is one where it is sensible for the governors to allow the headteacher some scope.

## MONITORING THE BUDGET

It is important to keep a careful eye on whether planned expenditure is on target or exceeding it. This applies more to the high cost items than to the low cost ones. If the expenditure on postage is 10 per cent over budget, this is hardly a disaster: if the staffing budget is, then that is very serious indeed.

The business manager or bursar should be fully involved in this process, providing the headteacher and other budget holders with regular accounts of how much they have spent. One difficulty that schools sometimes face is that some money has to be spent in a particular financial year within specific parameters. This applies especially to standards funds, although there is now some scope for carrying forward money to the end of August and/or viring it to other budget headings. It is much more difficult to recode expenditure after the event and therefore budget holders must understand clearly the importance of informing the administrative staff when items are to come from a specific budget heading.

## GETTING VALUE FOR MONEY

There are two key principles to be applied in getting value for money. One is to ensure that the school knows what it wants to achieve and constantly looks at ways of matching spending to these ends. The other is to control income and expenditure as carefully as possible.

The discussion has already considered a number of points in relation to getting value for money, and a large part of the book has made the point about matching expenditure to aims. Here some further points will be made about the control of expenditure and the generation of income.

### Saving here and saving there

The point has already been made that saving on staffing will release more money than saving on, for example, postage. However, once staff have been appointed, the scope for savings here is limited. With regard to expenditure on books and equipment, all budget holders should be encouraged to look for discounts. If a school can save 10 per cent on spending of, say, £30,000 that amounts to £3,000. That is a saving worth making. Sometimes direct savings are not possible, but one may be able to negotiate free training. Alternatively, a supplier of computer software may be willing to give a discount in return for the school agreeing to host other schools for demonstrations of it in use at some point in the future.

### Generating extra income

While schools should always be attempting to save money, thought should also be given to generating extra income. One needs to exercise due caution here. First of all, there are certain things that schools are not likely to want to do for money. Examples include giving out free samples of goods, encouraging children or their parents to make further purchases. Most schools are aware of this issue and act accordingly. Secondly, the amount of money generated by a particular activity may not justify the expenditure of time and effort, very often by staff who would be better off doing something of more direct educational benefit to the pupils.

There are some charities that are open to approaches from schools for financial support. They are not usually keen on supporting ongoing expenditure or paying for the cost of things that they might expect the school budget to cover. One-off purchases or events are more likely to be supported.

A number of public funding opportunities are available, but these are often very localized and may also depend on so-called 'matched' funding. European Union funding is available in certain areas (for example, Pathways) and the rules on matched funding sometimes allow at least some of the staff time to be taken into account. European funding is also available for activities that seek to link schools and countries together.

The government also makes amounts of money available through such initiatives as the Specialist Schools Programmes (directed at secondary schools but part of the money can be used to provide teaching and resources in neighbouring primary schools), the Beacon Schools Programmes, and so on. Current details of such initiatives can be found by searching on www.teachernet.gov.uk. One problem for urban schools is that the rules about becoming, for example, a specialist school mean that a large amount of cash needs to be raised and there are very strict limitations on what counts as matched funding. Inner-city areas do not always have large numbers of large firms with money to spare, although there are some national companies that may help out.

## DISTINGUISHING BETWEEN COST AND VALUE

The overall aims of schools are not usually expressed in shareholder terms, such as providing large dividends. It is important that this is borne in mind at all times. The purpose of the budget is to ensure that the school strives towards its targets for pupil achievement and well being. Sometimes it will make sense to go over budget – but not by too much! – if the case warrants it. The purpose is not to save money, but to use it as well as possible. Hoarding large amounts of money for some hypothetical rainy day is not to be recommended. Apart from anything else, it may encourage the government or the local education authority to believe that schools are being provided with more money than they need.

Sometimes money invested in making the school feel pleasant, providing high-quality staff training or paying for rewards linked to the school achievement system, may look like a cost to the school. If it is leading to the raising of aspirations and consequently of levels of achievement by pupils, it is not really a cost at all.

One final point: there is no reason why staff in schools should feel apologetic for spending taxpayer's money in doing one of the most important jobs in the country. They are investing hugely, not only their time but also their commitment, to ensure that all can have a happy and prosperous future. They should not have to do this in conditions that other professions would never tolerate.

9

# MANAGING THE SCHOOL BUILDINGS

The most important thing about a school is its ethos and many very good schools operate in less than perfect buildings. However, it is important that the management, and improvement, of the school buildings are both given due attention. We will look at both structural and staffing issues. It is important throughout this chapter to remember that the purpose of managing school buildings effectively is to contribute to the education of the pupils. This should always be borne in mind when making decisions about expenditure. Some schools involve the pupils to a greater or lesser extent in making at least some spending decisions (or, more accurately, making recommendations to the senior management of the school): this is possible with children of all ages and not just those nearing adulthood.

## REPAIRS AND MAINTENANCE

While it was once the responsibility of the local education authority, the upkeep of the school buildings is now the responsibility of the governors. If the building is in good condition, this can be a real benefit. However, many school buildings are in a very poor state of repair, particularly in inner cities, where vandalism over the years may have added to local authority neglect to provide the school with an environment in which it is very difficult to establish a positive ethos. Where the governors are in a position to take a longer-term view, their decisions in this area can contribute significantly to the creation of this positive ethos that everyone seeks.

### Inside or outside?

The first decision that often has to be made is whether to concentrate on the outside or the inside of the school. The outside of the school is clearly the aspect that is most often seen by members of the public, including the parents of prospective recruits. On the other hand, once the school doors have been passed, it is the state of the interior of the building that will have the major influence on the quality of education. Added to this, it is often the case that work to the outside of the building will cost much more than some of the work that one might like to carry out in classrooms and corridors.

Work on the roof is clearly important if the result of not doing it is that there are regular leaks in parts of the school. This not only destroys the paintwork, but also in many cases the work of pupils. This is a case where the (literal) drip-drip effect can have a very severe impact on morale. If the roof looks like a patchwork quilt, but does not leak, then it might be better to spend money on internal decoration than to replace the roof. In the long run, of course, a neglected roof will cause problems and this needs to be borne in mind.

## *The power of paint*

One should not underestimate the 'power of paint' in raising morale and, indirectly, raising educational outcomes. If one is financially careful, it is possible to repaint a number of classrooms relatively cheaply. If they are painted in a colour such as magnolia, this should then be supplemented with colour displays. The room then changes its outlook every time display work is updated. Incidentally, one can sometimes get discounts on painting by agreeing to one or two rooms being painted during term time. Contractors who specialize in working with schools often find a great demand for work during the school holiday periods. Staff will often be prepared to live with the minor inconvenience of doing without a classroom for a week or so during term time, if the result is that more renovation work can be done in the school. (Schools wanting work done during school holiday times should book contractors well in advance.)

With regard to the painting of corridors, it is worth considering having a darker paint up to about shoulder level, so that the inevitable rubbing of pupils' arms along the wall as they wait to get into a classroom does not make the corridor look scruffy. It also means that the caretaker can repaint half a wall instead of a whole one.

One point to note about painting toilets is that sometimes it is advised to use a flecked paint, which is supposedly vandal proof. However, it is very difficult to paint out any graffiti that does appear. Since toilets are used a lot in a school, it is probably necessary to have them painted as frequently as every summer holidays. This is a job that can be done by the caretaking staff and need only involve the purchase of some tins of paint. It goes without saying that any graffiti should be removed immediately and a serious attempt made to find the culprit(s). The point also needs to be made from time to time to the pupils that the toilets represent a facility for them and should therefore be looked after properly.

## Noticeboards

Attractive noticeboards can be inexpensive. For example, some schools arrange for simple boards to be put up in classrooms. These can then be painted in a suitable, plain colour, to act as a background for both pupils' work and learning resources. One useful tip is to check whether the ceiling of a particular classroom needs to be painted – ideally, of course, it would be, but it is not always essential to do so. Many classrooms now have a suspended ceiling, which means that painting is not necessary.

In corridors, it may be worth investing in some noticeboards with clear, lockable fronts. These encourage staff to be more proactive about putting high-quality work on display and they can add considerably to the learning environment. There are some contractors who specialize in working with schools, providing cost-effective solutions. It can sometimes be very expensive if one buys these boards through a catalogue intended for the corporate world of big business. The purpose of the board is to highlight what is in it, not the name down the side.

## Lighting and signs

It is also worth considering installing new lighting, particularly in corridors. Some of the lighting found in schools is quite old and is not necessarily effective. Internal signage can help create a purposeful atmosphere and is as important as the signs that appear outside the school.

## The cost of walking on floors

While the result of spending money on painting is usually very visible, that spent on the maintenance of floors is often viewed as money wasted. Many schools have at least some valuable floors – including woodblock ones – that need to be looked after very carefully. Since the primary purpose of a floor should be to stop one falling down a hole while getting from one place to another, maintaining such floors can often be seen to be an unnecessary drain on resources. However, from a psychological point of view, a good quality wood floor needs to look well; otherwise that part of the school can look very untidy and shoddy. It is probably sensible to have a complete refurbishment of such floors every few years or so, finance permitting. They can then be sealed in such a way that it is not too expensive to keep them looking reasonably well.

While laboratories and workshops may need specific types of flooring, for most general-purpose classrooms, one has to decide between carpet and vinyl coverings. Carpet can help with noise control, which is particularly important when oral work is increasingly seen as important for delivering the National Curriculum at all key stages. However, it can be fairly unforgiving, particularly with regard to marks made by mud and/or such substances as chewing gum. In the case of vinyl, there appears to be a movement away from individual tiles to using sheets, two or three of which may be enough to cover an average-sized room.

If the type of flooring in a room is going to be changed, the cleaners (or cleaning contractor) need to be made aware of this, well in advance, in case they need to purchase new cleaning equipment.

### Curtains and blinds

It is worth considering putting curtains and/or blinds in at least some classrooms. This can improve acoustics, make rooms feel more businesslike and stop the sun interfering with lessons. Different schools find that different solutions work for them; indeed, in some schools, different solutions work in different classrooms. It is vital that staff are made aware of the need to ensure that window coverings are not damaged.

It also needs to be borne in mind that curtains eventually fade and, unless they are very expensive ones, can begin to disintegrate under the power of the sun. On the other hand, they may not need to be regularly cleaned, particularly if thought is given to the colour purchased. Blinds are more likely to need regular cleaning, which needs to be budgeted for.

### Air-conditioning

It is worth considering the installation of air-conditioning in some rooms, particularly those that house computers. However, not only are air-conditioning units quite expensive to purchase, but their running and maintenance costs also have to be taken into account. It is probably essential to have air-conditioning in the room that houses the school network server(s).

### *Sticking doors and faulty locks*

It is easy for headteachers, in their office and with 'private facilities', to forget that some of the most aggravating things for a classroom teacher are likely to be doors that stick, or will not stay closed, and locks that do not work properly. There should be a reporting system for faults. The simplest way of doing this is to make a supply of pre-printed slips, on which staff can write out details of such faults and pass them to a member of the administrative staff for action. It can be useful to have two colours, one for urgent items (definition needs to be given, such as electrical, otherwise everything will become urgent) and non-urgent items. All faults should be dealt with as quickly as possible.

A regular note to staff, possibly every term but certainly at least annually, can ask for problems to be identified. They can then be rectified, possibly during a holiday period. It is absolutely vital that all staff, including teachers, are encouraged to take pride in the bit of the school in which they operate. Making sure that any defects reported are dealt with quickly is a good way of encouraging this sense of involvement.

In addition to this, a senior member of staff (at deputy or assistant headteacher level, possibly) should make regular checks of the school, accompanied by the caretaker and possibly the business manager. During these walkabouts, a note should be made of any defects that need to be dealt with immediately and any that need approval as part of a larger programme of work.

## CAPITAL WORKS

While the day-to-day repairs and maintenance are the responsibility of the school, more extensive capital work is a different matter. For the purposes of this chapter, it will be assumed that the school is a fully funded local authority one, but the points made will apply to virtually all schools, even if the funding arrangements can vary.

In recent years, schools have been given devolved capital, which allows at least some 'improvement' work to be carried out. Above a certain level of expenditure, however, it will be necessary to bid for a substantial amount of capital funding. We will look at major bids first, and then at how devolved capital can be used.

## Major works

It is the case that many schools need expenditure of millions of pounds to bring them up to a satisfactory state. To replace the flat roof of a medium-sized secondary school, for example, can easily cost in the region of £250,000. The replacement of heating systems, including pipe work, can easily cost in the region of £100,000. It can cost many thousands to resurface a defective playground area or to replace faulty windows. For work like this, large capital bids may be necessary.

The first thing for a school to do is to make a 'wish' list. This can be compiled by a group consisting of one or two governors, one or two members of the senior management team and the business manager. The job here is to list major repairs (the examples given earlier of heating systems, resurfacing of the playground and the replacement of the roof would fall into this category) and desirable improvements (for example, the creation of a new play area for the infant children, a new all-weather surface for the junior children, new workshops or laboratories, new building for the sixth form). Provided that the group realizes that this is a wish list, there is no reason why such ideas should not include the provision of a new Sports hall or a new Arts block. This list needs to be discussed with the local authority, particularly with regard to major repairs or projects. Even if they do not see the need for a new building, they should certainly be aware of heating, roofing and playground problems. The aims of the meeting should be: 1) to get the school on the list for these major repairs; and, 2) get advice on the rest of the wish list.

Lack of funding is usually the main problem, although in some cases the local authority may have plans for the school (for example, closure or the additional provision of special educational facilities) of which the school is currently unaware.

There are several key sources of funding for major projects. These include in some cases the availability of European or national government funding, often linked with urban regeneration projects. If the school is likely to be eligible for such funding, detailed plans will need to be discussed with various interested bodies. Such projects will almost certainly require some kind of joint use of the facilities.

The lottery can also fund various building projects. These will include in particular the provision of Arts and Sports' facilities. Schools that are prepared to put themselves at the centre of the community and open their doors to local people may find that they get additional facilities. Running costs need to be borne in mind when applying for such funding. However, if the school is prepared to cover these costs (caretaking, heating, lighting, and maintenance of grassed or all-purpose areas), they will often find that the local community is more than happy for the facilities to be added to the school. (More will be said about community involvement in the next chapter.)

Secondary schools are eligible to apply to be designated as specialist colleges, in such areas as Modern Foreign Languages, Technology, Sport, the Arts, and so on. If they are designated, they become eligible for a capital grant. It may be beneficial to link this programme of work to other projects.

Another source of funding for major projects (including the provision of entire new schools) is what is known as PFI: this is a joint public-private funding initiative. At present there are not many examples of such initiatives involving schools. They are usually set up to replace, say a primary school, with a brand new one. In return for the school being built, it is agreed that the private contractor is paid to maintain the building over a period of, say, 30 years. The maintenance could include cleaning, grounds maintenance, and so on. This does mean that the school hands over a large part of its annual budget for a long period of time. The private contractor may also, as part of the deal, be able to use the school outside normal school hours and weeks of work to run, for example, conferences or ICT training sessions. Any school considering a PFI bid needs to take expert advice on these matters.

## Devolved capital

Prior to the devolution of some capital funds to schools, many local authority officers adopted the motto, 'Safe, dry and warm', when making decisions about spending on small- or medium-size projects. This is a useful starting point for schools, when considering how to spend their devolved capital. It is not necessary to spend devolved money in the year in which it is allocated, which allows schools to roll money forward (albeit for a limited period of time) and spend more than one year's allocation on a larger project. It is also possible to spend in advance, subject to the agreement of the local authority.

Suitable projects include replacing damaged roofs, installing new boilers, repairing dangerous play areas, and so on. It is worth finding out what major projects the local authority is likely to support before deciding how the school will spend its devolved capital. There is no point in, for example, replacing a boiler if the local authority is actively considering some major expenditure in this area, possibly from a different pot of money.

One important point to bear in mind when carrying out capital work is the issue of future maintenance and running costs. It may be worth paying a bit extra up front if these extra costs can be recouped over a period of, say, 5 or 10 years through reduced running costs. It is very tempting not to worry about the future, but this is how school buildings ended up in their present state. Somebody has to take responsibility for the future, even if the personnel concerned in these spending decisions are not likely to be around when the chickens come home to roost!

## Small-scale improvements

Some schools are finding that they can put aside some money each year for small-scale improvements. It is always worth looking for ways in which this can be done. If, for example, the school roll increases, it might not always be necessary to spend the bulk of the extra money on extra staffing. The advantage of putting money into capital projects is that they are often one-off costs, unlike the employment of staff, which is almost certainly going to cost more with each passing year.

If, for example, a member of the office staff leaves at a slack time of the year, it might be worth not seeking a replacement immediately. The money thus saved could go towards the improvement programme. A similar thing can occur if a teacher or classroom assistant leaves at Easter.

### *Utilities*

It is always worth checking if the current costs of gas (or oil), electricity and water could be reduced. One needs to be sensible about this and be totally clear if savings are actually possible. For example, if electricity is charged on the basis of the maximum use during the day, it makes sense to look at this rather than have someone switching off lights during evening activities.

# STAFFING

Schools traditionally had one or two caretakers, with fairly general duties including opening and closing the school, doing some cleaning, possibly dealing with small repairs, notifying the local authority if work needed to be done, and so on. With the delegation of funding to schools, many have taken the opportunity to look at the whole range of needs and to try to create a staffing structure to reflect this.

Some larger schools have a site manager, who may have been senior caretaker previously or who may have been recruited specifically to the post. This person is then responsible for the fabric of the building, contact with contractors and possibly the management of one or more other staff.

The areas of responsibility that can be assigned to a site management team include opening and closing the school, security, supervision of areas of the school during breaks and lunchtime, painting and decorating, and carrying out some improvement programmes. If this view is taken of things, then it is possible to find the salary costs of such a team from such budget areas as overtime payments for lettings (employing an extra person with a different pattern of working hours may be possible), midday supervision, and repairs and maintenance. A good team that takes responsibility for the buildings and takes a pride in their achievements is worth having.

In the short term, this is not always possible. There are many practices that militate against the flexibility needed to work within such a team. Usually, any change can be aided by looking at salary structures and by sometimes making one-off payments if the team has been working particularly effectively.

## SECURITY

It is unfortunately the case that many urban schools suffer severely from various forms of criminal damage, including arson, theft and vandalism. While in many areas, the issue of security is not a major one and may well not involve the headteacher directly, in urban schools this is not so. There is no point in setting a vision and inspiring people to work towards achieving it if the sight that greets everyone on most Monday mornings is boarded-up windows, burnt-out cars and the remains of an attempt to burn the school down. The issue needs to be tackled. One bonus of making at least some headway in this matter is that staff will see that the headteacher is aware of the difficulty of working under such conditions and is trying to do something about it. Any success in this matter will also contribute to the feeling that progress is possible, and this may in turn influence belief in the possibility of raising educational achievement. There are no easy solutions to this problem and, indeed, it needs to be tackled on a number of fronts simultaneously. We will look at some things that can be tried.

### The school belongs to all

The first thing, which has no financial cost to it, is to convince people that the school belongs to the pupils and their community. In the next chapter we will look in more detail at community involvement, but here it is worth mentioning that any attempt to open the school to the community has potential benefits in persuading more people that the school is theirs and that they can help to look after it. Friendly neighbours keeping an eye on the buildings can nip trouble in the bud. They do not need to be identified – all that is needed is a call to the local authority security service or the police.

Pupils should also be involved in looking after the building. If vandalism during the school day can be minimized, this will make the place look better and will free money up to spend on other things. It is important to find ways of expressing costs arising from vandalism to the school in ways that the pupils can relate to and, in particular, to be specific about costs. The more directly they can see the benefits, the more likely they are to respond as one would wish them to. For example, the cost of repairing a damaged door can be expressed in resources for PE lessons. Withdrawing privileges if there is an act of vandalism can have some effect, if judiciously used. In some schools, there are few privileges to withdraw, so maybe some thought needs to be given to creating such privileges. Giving a school council a say in how a specified amount of money is to be spent can be useful. If there is wanton vandalism, then the amount needed to repair it can be taken from the 'pupil council fund'. This brings pressure to bear on the anti-social elements in the school.

It is also important that all staff realize that they can keep the school safer by closing windows at the end of the day, putting computers in designated secure areas, locking doors, making sure they do not lose their keys, and by keeping an eye out for any suspicious behaviour. They should never, of course, keep money or other valuables in school desks, since they are virtually inviting the opportunist thief to steal it or to pass information on to others.

## Designing out problems

Many schools were designed in the days when children would not willingly go near them unless they had to. Some thought the teachers lived there and were watching for miscreants! Those days have gone, but the buildings have not. Therefore, the first step to making the building secure is to look for nooks and crannies where bored teenagers can gather at night and to remove them. A doorway provides shelter from the elements, but it also attracts those who have nothing better to do. They may gather just to smoke or be with friends, but this can easily turn to dares on who will be able to break the most windows or start the most fires. Shutters of various kinds can be used or the corridor may be brought right out to the edge of the building. Computer rooms should be located on an upper floor if the layout of the school makes this possible.

## *Good fences*

It is generally accepted that schools need at least one fence to mark out the boundary. This at least makes a statement that what is included inside the fence belongs to the school and allows for the notion of trespass to arise. A boundary fence does not necessarily need to be high to serve this purpose, provided that any gates are closed and locked at night.

Occasionally, a right of way exists through a school, possibly on account of it being used unchallenged for that purpose over a number of years. Efforts need to be made – involving local councillors if necessary – to have something done about this. Sometimes, there may be solutions available to reroute the thoroughfare through a different part of the school grounds. Most reasonable people who use schools as a short cut do so because it saves them making a long detour: this is the audience at which one should be aiming any attempt at rerouting.

In addition to a boundary fence, most urban schools need a fence that acts as a deterrent to criminals, whether they are intent on causing vandalism, setting fire to the school or stealing property. Such a fence needs to be at least two metres high. There are two problems about this. The first is that it can be quite costly, although the savings in repairs and (especially) in morale can make it worthwhile to make this kind of investment. The government has made funds available to help with security measures and schools should seek to ensure that they appear on the list for future work. The second issue over security fencing is that it can make the school look more like a prison than a school. One has to offset against this the fact that if there is no fence, the school is likely to be the target of regular attacks. There are so many fences around buildings in urban areas that one may not look as out of place around the school as one fears. It is possible to have them painted in suitable colours (green is quite popular, although they still don't look like trees!) and to grow suitable vines or plants alongside them. If the latter is done, it is important to make sure that this does not just provide a climbing frame over the top of the fence. The fence needs to be checked regularly to make sure that any gaps are repaired quickly. If this is not done, then the fence will cease to serve any useful purpose.

## *Alarm systems*

A modern burglar alarm system is essential in every urban school. A fire detection system is also very valuable. It is usual now for such systems to be connected directly (by a dedicated telephone line) to the local authority security section and/or to the police. The system needs to be reliable if the police are to respond to it, which means giving careful attention to the siting of alarms. If there are ill-fitting windows, a windy night can lead to a poorly sited alarm being set off. At the very least this is inconvenient and will cost something in payments to the caretaker or security force.

There are mixed views on whether alarm systems should be silent or not. If they are silent, this gives time for a response to be made, and hopefully an arrest may follow. If they sound once disturbed by an intruder, this will often frighten off some criminals, although they may decide to vandalize the school on the way out.

## *Security cameras*

There is no doubt that well-sited and monitored closed circuit camera systems can be very effective at dealing with particular kinds of criminal damage. They are most effective at discouraging young vandals, for whom being caught on camera can lead to contact being made with their parents. Modern systems are also quite good at getting images that can lead to the identification of those who have been trying to break into the school. If the system is monitored, then a quick response can be made by a security service. A lot of damage is caused by young people who are not necessarily intent on stealing or setting fire to the school. In these cases, identification can help.

One point worth making about camera systems is that schools are often faced with a dilemma if a pupil is caught on camera. If a good working relationship exists with the police, it may often be better not to prosecute and to use this act of generosity to ensure that any further repetition is avoided. Once a pupil is expelled from school they not only are totally beyond the control of the school, but have just been given an added reason to want to attack the buildings.

## *Shutters*

There is a wide variety of security shutters available to schools. As with security fencing, some of them are far from pretty. However, those responsible for running most urban schools realize that their lack of beauty is compensated for by the fact that they help protect the school's working. Roller shutters are quite expensive but usually quite effective. If they are electrically operated, this adds to the cost. (It is important to allow for maintenance of roller shutters and to ensure that a 24-hour call-out service exists, in case one sticks in an open position on a Friday evening at around 6 pm!)

Various other kinds of shutters and window grilles can also be purchased, some of them internally fitted and some of them fitted into window frames. It is possible to have decorative patterns on permanent grilles, while others can be folded back during the day.

Different solutions may be appropriate for different parts of the building. Judgements have to be made on how likely a break-in is and what the ensuing damage is likely to cost.

### *Onsite and offsite security*

Some local authorities operate their own security service. The school should make regular contact with such a service and call them in for advice if there are any problems. Sometimes the release from prison of a local thief can lead to a spate of robberies. In this case, it may be useful to have static security positioned in one or more schools for a period of time.

If the caretaker lives on site, this can help stop some of the worst criminal acts. In this case, it can be useful to find ways of ensuring that it is not immediately apparent that they have gone out for the day.

During parents' and open evenings, it can be useful to organize things so that the caretaker is positioned in an area that helps ensure that the potential criminal is not offered an easy way into the school. Some schools have been burgled during such evenings when the alarm system has been switched off at the far end of the school. (If the alarm system can be 'zoned', this of course can help.)

### *Door entry systems*

Most schools now have some form of door entry system. Sometimes this is combined with a pass system, either by the use of locks that require a code to be entered to allow the door to be opened or by the use of pre-programmed cards. Care needs to be taken to change the pass number, as it is surprising how quickly pupils seem to be able to learn these! (Maybe there are lessons here for the numeracy strategy!)

If the door is not visible from the school office – and surprisingly few are – then a small camera can be mounted by the door, with a remote control button allowing someone in the main office to release the lock.

### *Eternal vigilance*

Ultimately it is only by everyone being vigilant that security, both during hours of opening and during nights and weekends, can be improved.

10

# THE SCHOOL AT THE CENTRE OF THE COMMUNITY

In many urban areas – and for many local communities – the local school represents the largest publicly funded resource. Schools are very often major employers of local people, particularly in the case of non-teaching staff and those who work for contractors (catering, cleaning and grounds maintenance, and so on). It is only right, therefore, that schools should endeavour to make their resources available to their local community, not forgetting at any time that their primary function is to educate the children on roll. Apart from this moral viewpoint, there are other reasons why schools should seek to become centres of their community.

There is plenty of evidence that schools that involve parents more closely in the education of their children find they are more positive about schooling. This benefits the children tremendously. There is also anecdotal evidence that parents who actively undertake further education themselves become very positive about ensuring that their children take full benefit of what is on offer. It is unfortunately the case that many parents in urban areas had poor experiences of school when they were young. If they can be attracted back into education themselves – for parenting classes, to catch up with literacy and numeracy, or to undertake some more advanced qualifications – they can see that schools really have changed. They then become more determined than ever to help their children do well.

Another advantage of encouraging community use of the school is that the longer it is open the longer a caretaker is likely to be on duty and the less likely it is to suffer from vandalism. If the school has a hall that can be let out – both primary and secondary schools have opportunities here – then the cost of caretaking, heating and lighting may be covered. In this case, any further activities may actually generate a profit, albeit one that is likely to be modest.

## THE SCHOOL AS A FORCE IN THE COMMUNITY

The enthusiastic school will find that there are lots of community groups that would like the school to nominate representatives for working parties, Pathways boards, and so on. The school should respond positively to these, particularly since many of the children attending the school will be affected directly or indirectly by the outcomes of some of these groups' activities. If the school is serious about being part of the community, it needs to become a real force within the community. It is often the case that people in urban communities feel that authority (for example, the housing department of the local authority) does not listen to them. Schools are in a very strong position to work with them and to help find the right places to target if they want action on matters that affect their daily lives.

## OFFERING ADULT EDUCATION CLASSES

It is not necessary to go through very detailed planning to become an adult education centre. All that are needed are some courses and people to attend them. The best way for a school to start is to think small. The headteacher and other members of the senior management team can take it in turns to act as centre manager (this would mean one week in three in a small primary school and one in six or seven in a large secondary school). The school then needs to find two or three teachers – preferably from the school itself – who are willing to offer two or three courses. ICT is always very popular, as are courses in English and Mathematics. Another popular choice is conversational classes in either Spanish or French. The teachers would be paid for teaching the classes, but the member of the senior management team on duty would be able to get on with other work; they might be given time off in lieu, if this is felt to be desirable. To start with, one night per week will allow the school to test out the viability of the exercise. Some subjects, such as ICT, may be able to subsidize others, so that smallish classes can be run for at least the first year.

Advertising can be done through parents and the local community. Once the demand has been established, local providers (especially local colleges of further education) can be approached to see if they are interested in becoming involved. Many of them can draw down funding related to widening participation. Since much of this funding is linked to recruiting adults from specific postcode areas, urban schools are often well-placed for this. The school may find that a local college is having difficulty meeting its targets and that it is more than happy to help run the night school. In some cases, the college will take it over, extend it to three or four nights per week, pay a centre manager, employ staff, advertise courses and pay the school rent for the hire of rooms.

## THE SCHOOL AS VENUE

Many local arts and music groups need a venue, to rehearse, put on shows or mount exhibitions. Such exhibitions can take the form of old photos from the area, maps of planned regeneration developments, and so on. The school should encourage this, as such activities can lead in all kinds of unforeseen directions. Local firms may on occasion be looking for a venue for training activities. This need not be large and the fee may only cover the school's costs. Nevertheless, the offer is worth making.

## PRACTICAL POINTS TO NOTE

The most important thing about becoming a genuine community school (and it is not essential to be designated as such to become one!) is to have a clear belief, allied to determination. It is also important to note that there are particular points to take into account. If they are not attended to, then the mission may become impossible.

### Care of the school

If different staff are using the school during the day and at night, then the centre manager needs to ensure that both groups are looked after. If possible, centre managers (who can be different people for different nights) should be daytime employees of the school. They can then find out if there are any problems – for example, a night school teacher removing work from the board or a daytime teacher never leaving any chalk for the night school – and move swiftly to deal with them.

Lettings for community events need to be planned in advance. It is a good idea to arrange for the business manager and/or one of the deputy or assistant headteachers to meet representatives of any group wishing to use the school for an event. It is also a good idea if someone calls in, if appropriate, while the event is taking place.

Cleaning may need to be reorganized if there are night-time classes as well as daytime ones. One option is to have the room cleaned twice, but the cheaper option is to move the cleaning of certain rooms to first thing in the morning. This needs to be arranged in advance, or little problems will grow into big ones.

## Adults and young people

Schools that operate evening classes find that young people are often on site at the same time as adult learners. This can be a very good thing indeed, but schools need to be aware that some issues may arise. Schools that operate study support in the evening will find 14-year-olds and 80-year-olds coming into school for different purposes. Even such simple matters as which toilets will be used (and will children use the staff toilets) can create problems, unless the issue is considered. There may also be child protection issues to be resolved. Refreshments may be needed. This may be done by providing machines or some parents may offer to run a tuck shop or coffee bar.

## Charging policies

Schools should aim as far as possible to offer free courses, particularly with regard to such basic skills as literacy and numeracy. As far as examination courses are concerned, it is often the policy to provide tuition free, with the candidate paying any examination fee. There is an argument that people do not commit themselves fully to courses that are totally free. On the other hand, some people can barely make ends meet. Each school needs to be aware of the issues and to deal with them as sensitively as possible.

## Funding

Urban schools often find it difficult to raise money from parents and in many areas there are no large employers who can help out. However, there may be opportunities to find the funding necessary to open the school from European sources (the European Social Fund, which mainly funds recurrent expenditure such as staffing, and the European Regional Development Fund, which mainly funds capital items). Some of the Excellence in Cities activities can easily be accommodated within schools after hours (particularly activities linked to the provision of extra opportunities for gifted and talented children and/or activities organized by learning mentors).

## MAKING MONEY OR MAKING SENSE?

The most important things for a headteacher who wishes to see their school become a genuine community school are threefold. First of all, there must be a clear vision of lifelong learning. Secondly, there must be a strong will and determination to overcome whatever obstacles are thrown up as the process starts. Thirdly, the question of money needs to be kept in perspective. The ambition is not to make money. Some money is needed to run the community activities, but it is not an objective in itself.

11

# DEALING WITH THE ENEMY

The theme running throughout this book is that urban schools need good leaders who have vision, enthusiasm and commitment. However, it is always well to keep an eye on those things that might hinder or derail attempts to create really effective urban schools. These things are characterized here as 'the enemy'. Once the 'enemy' is recognized, then it is easier to defeat it.

## SELF-DOUBT

The challenge of running a successful urban school is immense. It is not easy and sometimes it is very frustrating. At times, self-doubt may set in. It must not be allowed to take root. Hopefully, the injunctions throughout the book on ensuring that leadership is exercised at all levels and that a clear vision is shared throughout the school community will mean that when one person needs encouragement, there will be plenty of people there to supply it.

Headteachers need to believe that education is important and that it will make a difference to the lives of children. Leaders are expected to lead at all times, not just when the sun is shining. There is not time for self-doubt or self-indulgence. It is worth remembering the words of Abraham Lincoln, 'Behind the cloud the sun is still shining'. It can sometimes seem very cloudy in urban schools, but the sun does shine through from time to time!

The best antidote for times when things seem a bit more difficult than usual is to find a group of hopeful pupils and get strength from them. Sometimes a problem grows and grows within the confines of a room or a meeting. It is always advisable to do a 'reality' check on things. It is perfectly possible to exaggerate a problem or to 'deal' with a worse-case scenario that, when it comes to it, never actually happens. A school with a clear vision and leadership at all levels will be able to face the unexpected. It is just worth remembering that there is enough to do dealing with real problems, without worrying about ones that might arise in the future.

## CYNICS

One can take different views of cynics. Many of them started teaching with the same hopes and dreams that others did. Somewhere along the way they lost this, probably as a result of not being able to achieve what they thought they could. The challenge for every headteacher in every school is either to refire their enthusiasm (by showing that success can happen) or to at least ensure that they are so busy working they have no time to spread malaise among others.

Realism is not the same as cynicism, in spite of what cynics would sometimes like the world to believe. Realists accept that worthwhile achievements will not come on a plate or easily. They also recognize that in many cases it will often feel like a case of 'one step forward, two steps back'. However, for every child who fails to achieve, for example, a single GCSE, there are nearly 100 who do. That does not suggest that one should be complacent, but it does point up some of the successes of the educational system over the past two or three decades. Some thought that schools could not exist after caning was abolished, whereas in reality they are much better and more civilized places than they used to be.

The bottom line has to be that if someone is drawing a salary to do a job, they ought to do it. The alternative is to have the courage to do something else. No one is forced to teach.

## SO-CALLED EXPERTS

Teaching is beset by those who think that they know how to do the job better than those who are doing it day in, day out, in sometimes very tough circumstances. Sometimes these 'experts' may even have taught for a while, before finding something easier to do! Teachers instinctively know those who can offer really useful advice and who can support them in trying to be better tomorrow than they were today. There are some very good advisers and consultants who are helping urban schools work towards their ambitions.

However, a little humility would not go amiss with some of those who tell teachers not only what needs to be done but also how they should do it. Anyone can teach a demonstration lesson. The art of the teacher is not just teaching lessons but motivating and inspiring young people. This cannot be measured by adding up 'teaching grades' over a series of lessons.

Support for teachers needs to come from those who earn respect, by recognizing the qualities that every teacher has and by helping them improve on their practice. There does need to be constant improvement, but how this is achieved is very often a quite subtle process.

## THE POLITICIZATION OF EDUCATION

Reference has already been made to the fact that education has become something of a political football. The biggest problem about this is that the system encourages those who pass the public's money over to education to want to see very visible results over a relatively short period of time. (Incidentally, the money for education does not come from the Treasury: it comes from the public, including teachers!) This is not always possible and sometimes means that fairly meaningless measures are used.

There is another related problem that arises. If improvement has to be shown, then sometimes history has to be rewritten – or at least it has to start at a fixed time (for example, the date of the last general election). Any success has to be directly attributable to government actions, particularly with regard to the allocation of resources. Therefore, any rise in student performance (at, for example, GCSE) is not likely to be shown over a 20-year period, which would actually make more sense.

## A FINAL THOUGHT

This book started with a quotation from an Irish poet. The only thing that will change urban schools and hence change the lives of children is by headteachers and others taking action, by doing things, by moving forward. The book therefore finishes with an Irish proverb: 'You never plough a field by turning it over in your head'.

# APPENDIX 1

The following is an example of advice prepared for non-teaching staff on the management of pupils: it should be modified to suit individual schools. It is also useful advice for teaching staff when dealing with pupils outside the classroom.

**INTRODUCTION**

All staff are responsible for the good behaviour and friendly atmosphere of the school by the way in which they speak to, and deal with, children: non-teaching staff have a vital part to play in contributing to this ethos.

The basic rule for managing young people is that *respect breeds respect*. Our pupils are regularly told that all staff are to be treated with respect, in the same way that they themselves are treated by staff. There are very few instances of insolence to either teaching or non-teaching staff by the pupils. Any instances will be dealt with quickly and effectively.

**NOTES FOR GUIDANCE**

1. Children, like adults, generally respond better to consistent and quiet discipline than to being shouted at as if they are not also human beings. In a tense situation, it is often far more effective to lower one's voice than to raise it. Be careful not to become 'over familiar' with children, as this may compromise your ability to discipline them when necessary.
2. It is important that incidents are reported to the appropriate pastoral heads. We need this information to get a total picture of how children are behaving in school.
3. If you do not know the name of a child, ask for it. If they refuse to give it to you, make a mental note of what they – or anybody else present – look like. Pastoral staff are usually able to identify pupils from such a description.
4. It is easy to become annoyed if a child is being insolent but we are professionals and the public expect us to behave in a calm and reasonable way.

5. Do not shout at children, since there may be particular circumstances of which you are unaware, which could have very serious consequences.
6. Children in a classroom are the responsibility of the teacher in charge. You should not interfere with that responsibility by attempting to reprimand children. (This also applies when teachers are speaking to pupils outside lessons.)
7. Do not in any circumstances strike or grab hold of a child – or threaten to do so. Threatening to strike a pupil is an assault and actually doing so is battery. Such action(s) could result in a parent making a formal complaint to the school or to the police. It also makes it difficult to deal with the original offence.

Further help and support is readily available on request from [*deputy headteacher*].

# APPENDIX 2

The following advice relates to the issue of press releases by schools. It is followed by a hypothetical example.

**GENERAL ADVICE**

The first thing to bear in mind is that newspaper editors receive press releases all the time. In most cases the object of the exercise is to gain (free) publicity for the organization concerned, which in this case is the school. It is therefore important that the following points are borne in mind:

1. Finding out the name of the appropriate reporter or news editor can be useful. They can then be contacted prior to the press release, possibly to notify them that it will be on its way.
2. For most newspapers, a fax is usually more convenient than anything else, although in some cases they will be happy to accept an e-mail.
3. The story needs some point. Newspapers like unusual angles on a story. One school, for example, got good publicity for its OFSTED report by arranging for three generations of one family, a grandmother and mother who had previously attended the school and a daughter intending to attend in the future, to be photographed reading the report. This created a good photo opportunity for the local newspaper, which ran a nice feature on it. It is interesting to note that in this case the newspaper editor chose to send a photographer to the family home to take the photograph, rather than to the school.
4. It is important to keep stories to one side of A4, spaced at one-and-a-half lines, if at all possible. The first paragraph should summarize the story, the second one give a few short quotes, the next ones give more detail and the final one should give contact details. The person named here needs to be freely available (using a teacher is usually not a good idea, unless it is the headteacher, since the teachers are likely to be teaching when reporters ring back) and needs to be well-briefed on the story.

5. The fact that a story does not appear should not deter the school from sending further ones. It is also worth noting that the story may be used later, especially if it is not tied to a particular date. One other point to make is that many schools get their best publicity by sending in stories when there are not many school-focused stories around, particularly over the summer and Christmas holiday periods.
6. It is sometimes worth sending a good clear photograph, although often the newspaper will prefer to send their own photographer. If the latter is the case, it is always a good idea to have a small number of pupils available, all of whom should be in full school uniform. It is also a good idea to have areas both inside and outside the school that lend themselves to photographs being taken, preferably with the school name and/or logo in the background.
7. Note that the old formality of addressing headteachers as Mr or Mrs has been replaced by a less formal approach. It is now usual to put the headteacher's first name in a press release and for the reporter (who may be relatively young) to address the headteacher in a familiar way.
8. It is usually quite adequate to issue press releases on the school's headed notepaper, which has the added advantage of giving address, telephone number, fax number and Web site address.
9. A point worth noting about the sample given below is that copies of the paper were purchased and sent to the school in China. This was in addition to the usual copies being put around the school and sent out to governors.

## A SAMPLE PRESS RELEASE

**Press Release**
6 December 2003

The headteacher of [*full name of the school*] School, [*headteacher's full name*], has just returned from a week-long study visit to China. In total, the heads of 10 local schools went on the visit, which included meetings with local education officials and the British Council.

[*Headteacher's first name*] spent most of his time in [*name of Chinese school*] School, which is situated in the city of [*name of city*]. It is the intention that a close link will be established between both schools, leading to e-mail contact, teacher visits and pupil exchanges.

There is a great interest in China in learning English. [*Head's first and second names*] says: 'The demand for English teaching in China is immense. Every young person sees the need to learn English as China increases it trade with the rest of the world. There is also a great interest in studying at English universities. It is interesting to note there are now nearly 18,000 Chinese students in higher education in the United Kingdom.'

[*Headteacher's first name*] feels that teaching in a Chinese school is very different from teaching in the United Kingdom. 'For a start, class sizes are so much bigger.' He taught a class of 54 14-year-olds and even the sixth-form class he taught had over 40 in it. The school itself is much bigger, with 2,400 students (aged 13–18) on roll.

Teaching is more didactic than in this country and all the young people appear very keen to learn. They are very supportive of each other in class and readily applaud the efforts of their classmates. 'I even managed to persuade a 14-year-boy to stand up and sing in front of the whole class!' He added, 'I consider that I have been very privileged to spend this time at [*name of Chinese school*] School.'

Press queries to: [*Headteacher's first and second names*], on [*school number*] or [*headteacher's mobile number*]

ENDS

# APPENDIX 3

The following is intended to stimulate some thought on how a school development plan can be constructed, that starts from first principles, focuses on all-important outcomes and can be constructed in such a way that it is deliverable in the classroom. It is not intended to be a blueprint for every school.

It starts with an overall statement, in this case covering a period of four years. There is then a short commentary on some aspects of the overall aims. Finally, a grid is shown that is partly completed, indicating how the plan is presented to staff each year. Each teacher/subject area then indicates the actions to be taken by them to help meet the school aims, on a special set of forms.

[*Name of school*] SCHOOL
[*school motto*]

School Development Plan, 2003–2007

Our philosophy:

[*school philosophy*]

Our aim:

To provide the best education in the best possible learning environment

*By 2007 we aim to have*

PUPILS

*with*

| Personal qualities | Values | Qualifications, skills, knowledge |
|---|---|---|

*through*

CURRICULUM

| National Curriculum | Individual pupil needs |
|---|---|

*by*

STAFF

| Personal qualities | Values | Qualifications, skills, knowledge |
|---|---|---|

*in*

BUILDINGS

| Physical attributes | Learning environment |
|---|---|

*working with*

PARENTS & COMMUNITY

| Supporting children | Values | School as learning centre for all |
|---|---|---|

## PUPILS

*Personal qualities*

High self-esteem
Confident in own views – assertive, but not aggressive
Collaborative/cooperative
Conscientious
Reliable
Tolerant

*Values*

Care for others
Respect for others
Tolerance
Equality of all
Spirituality – value of human beings

*Qualifications, skills and knowledge*

Gain nationally-recognized qualifications, including GCSE and GNVQ
Accreditation of non-examination activities through a school Record of Achievement

## CURRICULUM

We will deliver the programmes of study required by the National Curriculum. In addition we will aim to meet individual needs by providing a range of other courses and activities, including pre-vocational ones.

## STAFF

Since young people learn from influential adults, the staff of the school will seek to embody the qualities and values expected from the pupils, as outlined above. They will lead by example. The school will identify the training needs of staff and will allocate resources to ensure the professional development of all staff.

## BUILDINGS

We believe that the provision of a first-class education needs buildings that are conducive to our aims. We will aim to create a first-class learning environment, insofar as resources permit.

## PARENTS AND COMMUNITY

We will work to ensure that parents and the wider community support us in developing the qualities and values in the pupils, which have been outlined above, preferably leading by example. We wish to provide opportunities for parents to contribute to their children's progress. We will also create learning opportunities for parents and other members of the local community.

Each priority will be the responsibility of a member of the Senior Management Team, set out to include the following:

- priority;
- key tasks;
- intended outcomes;
- person(s) responsible;
- resources allocated (including time, finance, support);
- target date(s) for implementation and review.

[*Name of school*] SCHOOL
[school motto]

School Development Plan, Priorities, 2003–2004

| **Priorities** | **Pupils** | **Curriculum** | **Staff** | **Buildings** | **Parents/ community** | **SMT** |
|---|---|---|---|---|---|---|
| 1. Develop high self-esteem among pupils | Councils | NC + PSHE | By example | Toilets, etc | | AA |
| 2. Develop respect for others among pupils | Councils | ✓ | By example | | | BB |
| 3. Manage the 'new' National Curriculum | | ✓ | ✓ | | | CC |
| 4. Develop pre-vocational and vocational courses | | ✓ | ✓ | | | DD |
| 5. | | | | | | |
| 6. | | | | | | |
| 7. | | | | | | |
| 8. | | | | | | |
| 9. | | | | | | |
| 10. | | | | | | |
| 11. | | | | | | |
| 12. | | | | | | |

# REFERENCES

Hay (2002) *No Barriers, No Boundaries: Breakthrough Leadership that Transforms Schools*, HTI, Coventry (copies are obtainable from The Vanguard Centre, University of Warwick Science Park, Coventry, CV4 7EZ, United Kingdom. Tel: +44 (0)2476 410104)

Rudd *et al* (2002) *High Performing Specialist Schools: What Makes the Difference?*, NFER, Berkshire, ISBN: 1 903880 24 6

# INDEX